PRAISE FOR
AGITATIONS: ESSAYS ON LIFE AND LITERATURE

Arthur Krystal is an elegant subversive, an "inside agitator" in the highest sense of the phrase. His *Agitations* are warmed and illuminated by the burning candor of a bookish man who—so he attests—has lost his appetite for books. His voice is companionable yet blunt, graceful but trenchant, and by turns learned, informed, witty. Best of all, he addresses serious questions with the tools of a true essayist: a ready heart, a sharp mind, and no preconception of the answers.

Finalist, The 2003 PEN Award for the art of the essay

Whether he is writing literary essays that wear their learning lightly or familiar essays that breathe the spirit of Montaigne and Hazlitt, Arthur Krystal's work is a pleasure to read: conversational in tone, casually provocative, and enlivened by apt metaphors and felicitous quotations...His paradoxical approach invites disagreement, but, to an astonishing degree, it gives us the flow and cadence of someone actually thinking.

Morris Dickstein

Krystal celebrates the author compelled to write by a sense of mortality and the critic qualified to judge literature by traits of temperament and taste ... And as his vibrant, well-considered essays reveal, Krystal has not entirely relinquished hope that "books, despite the critics' polemics, are still the truest expressions of the human condition."

Elizabeth Mary Sheehan, *The New York Times Book Review*

[Krystal] sees the activities of writing and reading as deeply connected to basic human questions of life, death, religion, value, and taste. In graceful, conversational prose, he both argues and demonstrates his points, easily combining his knowledge of history and philosophy with the personal to give readers a view of an engaged mind."

Library Journal

Arthur Krystal's amazing essays in *Agitations* restore intelligence, wit and sanity to the life of the mind. I regard it as a must for the teaching of the essay. Krystal makes literature dance again and ideas matter.

Barbara Probst Solomon

Agitations: Essays on Life and Literature is a bracing antitoxin to the politics and theory passing for criticism in today's academic world... Arthur Krystal's mind and style manage to flourish in a postmodern culture where literature has—in his fine phrasing—"become the center that is somehow beside the point. His short but rangy essays now make up a book that is uniformly stimulating and at times even noble.

Thomas Mallon

PRAISE FOR
THE HALF-LIFE OF AN AMERICAN ESSAYIST

Krystal's conversational prose is an instrument adaptable to subjects as light as laziness and as serious as sin. Wide reading and cogent arguments are leavened with wit, irony and striking turns of phrase—altogether what essays should be.

Jacques Barzun

It is a superb book, winning the rare literary trifecta of being well-written, well-reasoned, and well-researched. [The] essays are not only a pleasure to read one by one—they are a pleasure to read paragraph by paragraph.

Dana Gioia, Chairman of the National
Endowment for the Arts

Krystal makes a vigorous case for the virtues of old-fashioned literary criticism, twitting the navel gazers of "creative nonfiction," which he dismisses as just a fancy word for memoir: and he's not afraid of weighty topics: he slogs through the notebooks of Paul Valéry, ponders different theories of beauty and offers a defense of the seven deadly sins.

Matthew Price, *The New York Times Book Review*

Arthur Krystal's essays shine like a searchlight through the fog of contemporary culture. Vivid, sharp, and enlightening, they keep a steady keel through roiling waters. These essays are as exciting about such arcana as the history of the typewriter and eighteenth-century boxing as they are about universals such as money, laziness, and beauty.

Edward Mendelson, Lionel Trilling Professor of the Humanities, Columbia University

A well-crafted set of eclectic essays covering subjects ranging from the history of the typewriter, to ex-slave turned pugilist Tom Molineaux, to the Mid-Century Book Society. As with his previous work, his latest output derives its strength from Krystal's dry wit and his seeming inability to pull any punches…Whether you agree with him or not, this is refreshingly good stuff.

Library Journal

Reading Krystal on beauty, sin, typewriters, laziness, death, duelling or reading, one has no sense of what one is getting into—beyond something one feels impelled to get more deeply into…To read one Krystal essay is to become a Krystal reader, and to want more than his two fine books, *Agitations* and *The Half-Life of an American Essayist.*

Wyatt Mason, *Harper's Magazine*

Arthur Krystal is smart, keenly observant, death on pretension, and a prose writer of genuine style—qualities that combine to make him a superior essayist.

Joseph Epstein

When was the last time you settled in with a collection of essays and read straight through? … Literate, original, conversational, witty, allusive, written for an educated general reader, the dozen pieces brought together here range over an amazingly wide terrain … May the tradition of writing essays such as his never decay.

Joan Baum, WLIU Radio

Whether writing on topics such as beauty, sin or laziness, literary essayist Arthur Krystal embodies the very best of what the essay should be: informative, interesting and eclectic. Elucidating his subjects by way of his literary yet accessible style, his refreshingly snarky wit shines through in a way that's completely endearing.

Bibliobuffet

Arthur Krystal is the George Clooney of the essay world, with his debonair vocabulary, utilization of complex yet lucid sentence structure, spot-on pacing, and an understanding of the history of the essay.

The Adventures of the Garbageman's Daughter

EXCEPT WHEN I WRITE

EXCEPT WHEN I WRITE

REFLECTIONS OF A RECOVERING CRITIC

ARTHUR KRYSTAL

OXFORD
UNIVERSITY PRESS

OXFORD
UNIVERSITY PRESS

Oxford University Press, Inc., publishes works that further
Oxford University's objective of excellence
in research, scholarship, and education.

Oxford   New York
Auckland   Cape Town   Dar es Salaam   Hong Kong   Karachi
Kuala Lumpur   Madrid   Melbourne   Mexico City   Nairobi
New Delhi   Shanghai   Taipei   Toronto

With offices in
Argentina   Austria   Brazil   Chile   Czech Republic   France   Greece
Guatemala   Hungary   Italy   Japan   Poland   Portugal   Singapore
South Korea   Switzerland   Thailand   Turkey   Ukraine   Vietnam

Copyright © 2011 by Arthur Krystal

Published by Oxford University Press, Inc.
198 Madison Avenue, New York, New York 10016

www.oup.com

Oxford is a registered trademark of Oxford University Press

Library of Congress Cataloging-in-Publication Data
Krystal, Arthur.
Except when I write : reflections of a recovering critic / Arthur Krystal.
p.   cm.
Includes bibliographical references and index.
ISBN 978-0-19-978240-6 (cloth : acid-free paper) 1. Criticism. 2. Literature and society.
3. Learning and scholarship. I. Title.
PS3611.R96E93   2011
814'.54—dc22   2011016137

1 3 5 7 9 8 6 4 2

Printed in the United States of America
on acid-free paper

CONTENTS

AUTHOR'S NOTE

In the first essay of this book, you will find a line that Edgar Allan Poe attributes to Montaigne: "People talk about thinking, but for my part I never think except when I sit down to write." The sentence made me both smile and wince because I knew immediately that in my case it was incontestably true. I seem to walk around having thoughts of no particular merit or originality, yet when I sit down to write, my imagination swings into action and suddenly my mind teems with expressive conceits and articulated phrases that otherwise would remain dormant. Perhaps one instance will suffice.

When writing about the poet Paul Valéry, I began to wonder how such an intelligent and self-contained man could be at the same time an artist and an anti-Dreyfusard. Although Valéry was a traditionalist and a reservist in the army, he was anything but a camp follower. He pronounced judgment on both the Left and the Right, identifying precisely the faults of each. But knowing this about Valéry does not explain what led me to write "his own striking example of the intensely private individual functioning in the public realm illustrates a simple truth: The individual cannot be more important than the state if the state is to survive, but if the state is to survive *honorably*, then the *idea* of the individual must be more important than the *idea* of the state." I make no great claims for this observation. For all I know, it, or some variation of it, may have appeared a dozen times before. What I do know is that it was a very unlikely thought for someone like me to have; politics is not my forte.

Another man I write about is William Hazlitt, and he wore his politics on his sleeve. Hazlitt is a writer I like and admire, and he, too, was a lot smarter in print than in person. In his wonderful essay "The Fight," Hazlitt recalls overhearing one man say to another, "Confound it, man, don't be insipid" and thinking, "that's a good phrase." It is a good phrase. I said it to myself once or twice while working on these pieces, and if I have failed only once or twice in heeding the admonition, I shall consider myself fortunate.

ACKNOWLEDGEMENTS

At 198 Madison Avenue: Shannon McLachlan
At 4 Times Square: Henry Finder and Leo Carey
At 620 Eighth Avenue: Jennifer Schuessler
At 666 Broadway: Jennifer Szalai
On the Upper West Side: Pam Dailey and Joy Adzegian
In the Bronx: Dasha Kiper

EXCEPT WHEN I WRITE

1

WHEN WRITERS SPEAK

That's Vladimir Nabokov on my computer screen, looking both dapper and disheveled. He's wearing a suit and a multi-buttoned vest that scrunches the top of his tie, making it poke out of his shirt like an old-fashioned cravat. Large, lumpish, delicate, and black-spectacled, he's perched on a couch along-side the sleeker, sad-faced Lionel Trilling. Both men are field-ing questions from a suave interlocutor sporting a B-movie mustache. The interview was taped sometime in the late 1950s in what appears to be a faculty club or perhaps a television studio decked out to resemble one. The men are discussing *Lolita*. "I do not . . . I don't wish to touch hearts," Nabokov says in his unidentifiable accent. "I don't even want to affect minds very much. What I really want to produce is that little sob in the spine of the artist-reader."

Not bad, I think, as I sit staring at the dark granular box on my YouTube screen. In fact, a damned good line to come up with off the cuff. But wait! What's that Nabokov's doing with his hands? He's turning over index cards. He's glancing at notes. He's *reading*. Fluent in three languages, he relies on prefabricated responses to talk about his work. Am I disap-pointed? I am at first, but then I think: writers don't have to be brilliant conversationalists; it's not their job to be smart except, of course, when they write.

Nabokov eventually dispenses with the cards; he can handle anything the interviewer throws at him, and yet his words don't shimmer, they don't settle in the mind with that incandescent pop one hears when reading his sentences. So, yes, I am a little disappointed even though I know that novelists, playwrights, and poets aren't always the best expositors of their own work. In fact, many of them come off as—well, ordinary. William Hazlitt, that most self-conscious of writers, was, by all accounts, not esteemed for his social graces, but made no apologies for it. "An Author is bound to write—well or ill, wisely or foolishly," he asserts in "On the Conversation of Authors". "But I do not see that he is bound to talk, any more than he is bound to dance, or ride, or fence better than other people. Reading, study, silence, thought are a bad introduction to loquacity." Hazlitt's argument is simple: "A lord is no less amorous for writing ridiculous love-letters, nor a general less successful for wanting wit and honesty. Why then may not a poor author say nothing, and yet pass muster?"

Saying nothing isn't the problem; it's saying or doing *anything*. According to Hazlitt, writers aren't fit for much besides writing: they don't wear clothes well, they eat sloppily, they don't even know how to greet people. The poor author is "too refined for the vulgar, too clownish for the fashionable . . . Introduce him to a tea-party of milliners' girls and they are ready to split their sides with laughing at him." Hazlitt probably felt he wasn't exaggerating, which tells you something about his own carefree sprint through life. But is he convincing? Not entirely.

Writers speak well enough, thank you, and not all women collapse into giggles on first meeting me. I do think, however, that writers who impress you on the page may not necessarily impress you in person. Conversational fluency isn't a writerly trait and unless the writer is a man or woman about town, someone at ease in all social situations—Somerset Maugham and Louis Auchincloss come to mind—he or she may flop around helplessly at dinner parties, gasping for conversational oxygen. Even W. H. Auden, no slouch when it came to graceful banter, felt the pressure: "Literary gatherings, cocktail parties and the like, are a social nightmare because writers have no 'shop' to talk . . . The literary equivalent of talking shop would be writers reciting their own work at one another, an unpopular procedure for which only very young writers have the nerve."

Me, I'm not so young; in fact, I was never that young, and unlike Hazlitt I feel somewhat abashed at not being a good public speaker—which nowadays, alas, means speaking to the media. A writer doesn't just write, he—if the publisher can swing it—goes on radio and television to hawk his wares. This entails dealing with trained personnel who know how to use their instruments: their voices, I mean. Everyone on the radio seems to have a melodious voice, a voice that doesn't break a sweat, a voice that makes my own voice sound as if I'd been gargling with sand. Have you noticed that broadcasters don't enunciate their consonants? I don't know about you, but my *b*'s and *p*'s *b*urst from my mouth like *p*ellets from a scattergun. And why does my voice shift out of gear for no discernible reason, stalling, jerking forward, racing, then stalling again? To hear yourself on radio is to wonder why anyone has ever slept with you.

Then, of course, there is everything you said that you wish you hadn't or wish you'd said better. That's the thing about conversation: you get only one crack at it. You can rephrase, qualify, even change direction, but it's doubtful that you'll ever get it just right. When speaking, each of us is a work in progress, shaped in part by those we're speaking to. One can be witty and occasionally even wise, but it's really not up to us: basically, we're only as good as our audience makes us. And even when we're in good form, tossing off Shavian quips and Orwellian pronouncements, the subject of our own novels or poems or personal essays may cause us to grope forward like larvae on a stick. What most people who attend readings don't grasp is that writers have no reason (other than a purely commercial one) to talk about their work. We talked about it when we wrote it. It's done.

Which doesn't necessarily mean that we know *what* we've done. On the YouTube clip, Nabokov maintains that he bred *Lolita* in his laboratory, that it was an exercise in craft, that he meant neither to shock nor awe. But Trilling doesn't buy it. Leaning forward and gazing down at the cigarette in his hand, Trilling cautions, "We can't trust a creative writer to say what he has done; he can say what he has meant to do—anyway, we don't have to believe him." Most writers, I think, realize this. All our carefully thought-out plans cannot guarantee how others will read us.

But that's not the point. We work in private so that our books can take our place in public. On the page we can be eloquent, dashing, smart, we can be *interesting*. And when it's done—the poem, novel, or essay—it becomes the face we want others to see, the voice we want them to hear, the person we want everyone to know. "You may rely on it," Thoreau assured his readers, "that you have the best of me in my books, and that I am not worth seeing personally, the stuttering, blundering clod-hopper that I am. Even poetry, you know, is in one sense an infinite brag and exaggeration. Not that I do not stand on all that I have written—but what am I to the truth I feebly utter?"

That's David Foster Wallace in white shirt and red tie talking to Charlie Rose on my computer screen. He has a white kerchief bundled around his head, from which strands of blondish hair drizzle down to his shoulders. The conversation ranges over teaching, movies, writing, and tennis. Wallace, the author of the intimidatingly erudite novel *Infinite Jest* and dozens of smartly written articles and essays, doesn't seem very intimidating. What he seems, for the most part, is pained by the thought that he's on television. "You're seriously asking me for my view on *The English Patient?*" he asks Rose incredulously. His disbelief is genuine; so is his discomfort. He knows that whatever gets said stays said, preserved in digital format, and it worries him. "A lot of this is going to get cut out, right?" he says hopefully a little later. Rose isn't trying to make Wallace uncomfortable; Wallace is sufficient unto himself. He's the very writer Hazlitt rose up to defend, except that Wallace, when he's not flagellating himself, speaks eloquently on almost any subject. He's also keenly aware that his discomfort is the price one pays for being a "library weenie." "Writing for publication is a very weird thing," he explains earnestly, "because part of you is a nerd . . . another part is the worst ham of all. . . . You want to stay in a library and the other part wants to be celebrated."

The interview occurred twelve years ago and Wallace, who committed suicide in 2008, became more poised in front of audiences as the demand for his presence increased. But I don't think he ever got really used to it, which is one reason that I liked and respected him. Show me a poet or novelist who talks glibly about his own work and I'll show you a writer who's said the same words a hundred times before. Nor am I forgetting about all the great writers who could talk a blue streak. If Dr. Johnson, Coleridge, Wilde, or

Shaw were alive today, the airwaves would be infinitely more interesting. The British critic Desmond MacCarthy, another excellent writer, was even more famous as a conversationalist. His son-in-law Lord David Cecil described him as "a supremely good talker, one of the few supremely good talkers I have ever met and equal to the best of them. In a charming, expressive voice, male and unmannered but beautifully modulated to convey his ever-changing shades of thought and feeling, his discourse flowed forth, relaxed, leisurely, enthralling."

Although I know no one who sounds like this, I'll concede there are plenty of writers around who, for reasons that are beyond my temperamental range, adore talking about their books and do so gracefully. The late John Updike was such a writer and his spoken words sometimes had the joyous fluency of his written ones. The Brits are still the best at marrying literary discourse to marketing, and I doubt that Martin Amis and Ian McEwan disappoint those who come to hear them. And yet I can't help feeling that the content of their conversation is on a par with the content of their work. They don't disappoint because their novels don't lead us to expect a Tolstoy or a Proust, who, I'm willing to bet, *would* disappoint should either pop up on Larry King.

Hazlitt was right about one thing: a writer creates expectations about his powers of speech, and the more the writer impresses us on the page, the greater we believe those powers to be. This is patently unfair—especially where young writers are concerned. A first-time author entering the public arena is an immigrant, a newbie. Unpracticed at the art of putting himself over, he or she may appear arrogant, foolish, and insecure. And even those writers who are old hands at the publicity game may not succeed in living up to their books. All their poise, eloquence, and wit may simply not be enough for besotted readers who presume a synchronicity between author and book. Hence, the reason for Hazlitt's not wanting to meet great writers: "We often hear persons say, What they would have given to have seen Shakespeare! For my part, I would give a great deal not to have seen him, at least, if he was at all like any body else that I have ever seen." My belated apologies, therefore, to Jorge Francisco Isidoro Luis Borges, whom I went out of my way to see and hear and who, at the time, left me feeling vaguely dissatisfied. How could it have been otherwise? I was holding him to a standard only his stories could achieve.

Thirty years ago I stood with a friend in the Metropolitan Museum of Art staring at Van Gogh's chalk and gouache painting *A Corridor in the Asylum*. Without looking away, I said, "Who does this remind you of?" He replied in under two seconds: "Kafka." For the sake of argument, let's say that my friend knew me well enough to know what I might have been thinking. In this case, however, he *also* felt that something about the painting was Kafkaesque. Something about the skewed receding hallway in which a solitary man is turning to the left, rendered in tints of brown, green, and yellow, seems to denote both loneliness and confusion. Whatever it was that made the painting evoke Kafka's name also suggests that Kafka's voice implanted in us a certain feeling or expectation about him. In fact, I suspect that more than a few readers will have a similar response to the painting, and I'd give odds that a multiple-choice question (Conrad? Hemingway? Waugh? Kafka?) would have many readers putting a check beside the Czech.

Vincent Van Gogh's *A Corridor in the Asylum*

I may be assuming too much here, but it seems to me that readers almost necessarily form an impression of the author. The impression will be vague and without physical particulars, but a persona does emerge from the tone and shadings of a voice. If you've ever spent a long time on the phone with someone you've never met, you know that a person takes shape even if you don't bother to calibrate his height or delineate her features, which is why it's usually a shock when you do meet for the first time. But what about those nice photographs of the author on the book jacket? Well, yes, there he or she is, perfectly lit, and usually looking trim, but isn't it true that while we're reading we don't see the person in the photograph? Instead, we're imagining without visualizing someone who seems to embody the bodiless voice.

Readers will recall that on page 26 of his *Introduction à l'analyse structurale des récits*, Roland Barthes put it in a nutshell: "He who speaks is not he who writes, and he who writes is not he who is." And therefore—well, actually, there is no therefore. We can't infer anything about anyone from how he or she writes. Did Cyril Connolly seriously believe that "it should be possible to learn as much about an author's income and sex-life from one paragraph of his writing as from his checque stubs and his love letters?" Connolly, I think, was just riffing on our natural tendency to equate the author with his work. We all do it. We read and make assumptions about the author's character. Philip Roth must be a self-absorbed, sex-obsessed Jew, since he writes about a writer who is both, and Nabokov must have been sexually drawn to prepubescent girls. Readers forget that skillful writers are in their own way actors, slipping in and out of roles as smoothly (and scarily) as Meryl Streep or Alec Guinness. And because we tend to confuse actors with their roles, we're disappointed when the actual author shows up in the flesh and turns out to be a nebbish. No wonder that Salinger kept to himself and Pynchon continues to stay out of sight.

Just so there is no confusion: I am not taking sides either with Sainte-Beuve, who claimed one has to know the details of a writer's life in order to understand the work, or with Proust, whose position may be inferred from his little book *Against Sainte-Beuve*. For Proust, "a book is the product of a different *self* from the self we manifest in our habits, in our social life, in our vices." Indeed, the essence of the writer, Proust maintains, is *limited* to the artistic work; it is not found in his conversations or even his letters. Frankly, I'm not sure that I see the need for argument here. Obviously, the life sheds light on the work; just as obviously there is an element of the work that springs from the writer's innermost self, which exists apart from that other, more superficial self. Writers tend to keep the Id at home, where it belongs.

Like most writers, I seem to be smarter in print than in person. In fact, I am smarter when I'm writing. I don't claim this merely because there is usually no one around to observe the false starts and groan-inducing sentences that make a mockery of my presumed intelligence, but because when the work is going well, I'm expressing opinions that I've never uttered in conversation and that otherwise might never occur to me. Nor am I the first to have this thought, which, naturally, occurred to me while composing. According to Edgar Allan Poe, writing in *Graham's Magazine*, "Some Frenchman—possibly Montaigne—says: 'People talk about thinking, but for my part I never think except when I sit down to write.'" I can't find these words in my copy of Montaigne, but I agree with the thought, whoever might have formed it. And it's not because writing helps me to organize my ideas or reveals how I feel about something, but because it actually *creates* thought, or, at least, supplies a Petri dish for its genesis.

The Harvard psychologist Steven Pinker, however, isn't so sure. In an e-mail exchange, Pinker sensibly points out that thinking precedes writing and that the reason we sound smarter when writing is because we deliberately set out to be clear and precise, a luxury not usually afforded us in conversation. True, and especially true if one writes for magazines where nitpicking editors with expensive shoes are waiting to kick us around for every small mistake. When people who write for a living sit down to earn their pay they make demands on themselves that require a higher degree of skill than that summoned by conversation. Pinker likens this to mathematicians thinking differently when proving theorems than when counting change, or to quarterbacks throwing a pass during a game as opposed to tossing a ball around in their backyards. He does concede, however, that since writing allows time for reveries and ruminations, it probably engages larger swaths of the brain.

I agree. I'm willing to bet that more gray matter starts quivering when I sit down to write than when I stand up to speak. In fact, if you were to do an M.R.I. of my brain right now, you would see regions of it lighting up that barely flicker when I talk. How do I know this? Because I'm *writing*! In fact, I'm so smart right now that I know my cerebral cortex is employing a host of neurons that are cleverly and charmingly transforming my thoughts and feelings into words. But if I were talking to you about all this, a different set of neurons would be triggered, different connections and associations would be made, and different words and phrases would be generated. In short, I'd be boring the pants off you.

O.K., I'm just guessing, but I do think that whoever wrote that he never thinks except when he sits down to write was using hyperbole to make a valid point. There's something about writing, when we regard ourselves as writers, that affects how we think, and, inevitably, how we express ourselves. There may be no empirical basis for this, but if, as some scientists claim, different parts of the brain are switched on by our using a pen instead of a computer—and the cognitive differences are greater than what might be expected by the application of different motor skills—then why shouldn't there be significant differences in brain activity when writing and speaking?

Along these lines, it seems that composers sometimes pick up different instruments when trying to solve musical problems. It's not that a violin offers up secrets the piano withholds, but that the mind starts thinking differently when we play different instruments. Or maybe it's just that the flow of thought alters when we write, which, in turn, releases sentences hidden along the banks of consciousness. There seems to be a rhythm to writing that catches notes that ordinarily stay out of earshot. At some point between formulating a thought and writing it down falls a nanosecond when the thought becomes a sentence that would, in all likelihood, have a different shape if we were to speak it. This rhythm, not so much heard as felt, occurs only when one is composing; it can't be simulated in speech, since speaking takes place in real time and depends in part on the person or persons we're speaking to. Wonderful writers might therefore turn out to be only so-so conversationalists, and people capable of telling great stories waddle like ducks out of water when they attempt to write.

So the next time you hear a writer on the radio or catch him on the tube or find him sitting beside you at dinner, remember he isn't the author of the books you admire; he's just someone visiting the world outside his study or office or wherever the hell he writes. Don't expect him to know the customs of the country, and try to forgive his trespasses when they occur. Speaking of dinner, when the German naturalist Friedrich Humboldt told a friend, a Parisian doctor, that he wanted to meet a certifiable lunatic, he found himself seated a few days later between two men. One was polite, some-what reserved, and didn't go in for small talk. The other man, dressed in ill-matched clothes, chattered away on every subject under the sun, gesticulating wildly, while making horrible faces. When the meal was over, Humboldt turned to his host. "I like your lunatic," he whispered, indicating the talkative man. The host frowned. "But it's the other one who's the lunatic. The man you're pointing to is Monsieur Honoré de Balzac."

2

CARPE NOCTEM

A Little Night Music

A man has written a book about the night. Well, why not? In the past decade or so, we've seen books on pencils, bookshelves, tobacco, cod, salt, spice, blood, bread, caffeine, crying, the penis, the breast, boredom, smiling, the hand, and masturbation. (Do the last six items seem to nudge one another?) Eventually, such books, and others like them, will all come to dust, including the two so far on dust itself, but before they do we might ask ourselves if this expenditure of print on the obvious and quotidian constitutes anything like a trend, or even a cultural shift.

These longish narratives, after all, deal with subjects that an English man of letters in 1820 might have devoted, at best, a dozen pages to. While grand abstractions (beauty, genius, the sublime) often produced long word counts, the smaller, more familiar aspects of life (vulgarity, idleness, getting up on cold mornings) were the domain of miniaturists like Lamb, Hazlitt, Stevenson, and, closer to our own day, Logan Pearsall Smith, or Cyril Connolly in one of his lighter moods. The thought that such matters required ventilating at book length would never have occurred to writers, much less publishers.

If it seems that any noun in the dictionary can be tricked out as a book these days, it's because the minutiae of daily life has acquired some intellectual capital. Good micro-histories do brisk business because they see the big picture in the smallest details, offering the hope that everything under the sun has meaning. So, whatever was formerly neglected, or looked at but not really seen—utensils, foodstuffs, or the hemp that was used to make the ladders that enabled enemies to scale the walls that housed a king—now demands the academy's respect and scrutiny.

It follows, then, as the night the day, that the night should have its own day. In fact, it's surprising that it's taken this long. One reason for the delay may be that A. Roger Ekirch, who teaches Early American History at Virginia Tech, took twenty years to research and write *At Day's Close: Night in Times Past*. Ekirch, if the Notes at the back of the book are any indication, has consulted what look to be a thousand and one sources, many of which puncture Thomas Middleton's elegant rendering of the night as fit for "no occupation but sleepe, feed, and fart." For Ekirch, the night—even before public lighting, mass transportation, and the introduction of official police forces changed it forever—has been a hubbub of activity, a sequence of comings and goings, a bustling fiefdom with its own distinct customs and rituals.

Today, those who live far from the tips of the earth, where it is continually night half the year, rarely find themselves in the dark. Unless you're hacking your way through jungle or humping along in the desert, some form of artificial lighting, either a light bulb or an L.E.D. (light-emitting diode), is sure to be nearby. Electric light is so much a staple of modern life that we forget that there are people around whose parents relied on only two sources of light: the sun and fire. Thomas

Edison's bright idea of 1879 notwithstanding, many homes, until the second or third decade of the twentieth century, were lit by small flames burning in gas lamps. In terms of radiant power, then, the Dark Ages lasted a lot longer than you may have thought.

How dark was it? Let's put it this way: an electric current coursing through a tungsten filament in a small glass vacuum produces a hundred times the light emitted by a candle or oil lamp. And, considering that no European cities deployed any kind of public lighting before 1650, the world at night was no place to take a stroll. Moonless nights presented a darkness so complete that anyone bold enough to step into Shakespeare's "vast sin-concealing chaos" was at risk of losing his footing, his purse, and his life. Carriages tumbled into ditches; houses were broken into or set on fire; and town squares filled up with beggars, prostitutes, crooks, and the crooked. In many cities, gangs roamed the streets. In 1606, a gangbanger by the name of Caravaggio killed a rival in Rome and fled to Naples. In London, young rakes, with such high-sounding names as the Scowrers, the Mohocks, and the Hectors, staked out territory and busted heads. (It's the street gang, not the noble Trojan, to which we owe the verb "to hector.") As Ekirch sees it, the night was "a forbidding place plagued by pestilential vapors, diabolical spirits, natural calamity, and human depravity." No wonder that an Italian proverb admonished, "Who goes out at night looks for a beating."

But people did go out, and they did so despite the warnings of the Church and city councils. Come dusk, bells were rung, horns were blown, and drums were beaten; city gates were shut, drawbridges raised, and stragglers forced to scurry home to light candles and tend the hearth. In medieval France, and throughout Europe, strict curfews were imposed. Around eight or nine in the evening, a bell sounded to indicate the *couvre-feu*, or putting out of fires, from which the word "curfew" derives.

To make the night even less hospitable, city officials saw to it that chains and logs blocked off major thoroughfares, and that crimes committed after curfew met with stiff penalties. When a woman of Siena was found guilty of assault in 1342, her punishment was halved because she had attacked a man, then doubled because she had hit him in his home, and then doubled again because the infraction had occurred at night. In some Swedish cities, a robbery committed after the curfew bell warranted the death penalty. In many European jurisdictions, killing a housebreaker was legal if the crime occurred at night but not after sunrise.

Yet, for many people, notably women and the indigent, the night was just another sunless day. The poor stayed up late, husking corn, spinning wool, boiling sap, and pounding rice. Servants and women knitted, wove, washed, and carded wool. Farmers and fishermen often worked past sundown, and on the dark streets a few grim-looking men emerged to dispose of dead bodies, empty underground cesspools, and clean up after the horses and cows. Indeed, some people have always worked at night, ever since the first sentry took up his post in Mesopotamia three thousand years ago. In time, most towns and cities instituted a night watch, consisting of either a single man or a patrol, whose duties were to discourage thieves, keep a sharp eye out for fires, and make sure that doors were locked. The job didn't pay much, and it attracted the sort of people you didn't want to meet at night. When they weren't shouting out the hour at the top of their lungs, banging on doors, and rudely accosting people, watchmen drank, shirked, and consorted with prostitutes and thieves.

Parisians called them *tristes-a-pattes* (flatfoots), and the English—witness Constable Dogberry in *Much Ado About Nothing*—also poked fun at them.

Properly speaking, a history is an evolving narrative concerning a person, a place, or an idea that has left consecutive traces over time (a syntactical nicety ignored by titles that promise "histories" of dust or the smile). One can write a history of comedy but not of laughter. Ekirch believes that he's writing "the history of nighttime in Western society," but that would imply that someone else could do the same for the morning or for three in the afternoon. What he's writing, of course, is a history of Western society during the nighttime, which, judging from the Notes, involves scanning every work of literature, sermon, letter, diary, newspaper, song, folktale, and instructional pamphlet, as well as every court, church, and medical record, that mentions the night. *At Day's Close* may not be an old-fashioned history, but it's among the few books, aside from annals of technology, to anatomize the incremental attempts to illuminate the darkness.

Man began with flint and wood and moved on to torches and candles—tallow, wax, beeswax, and spermaceti, the fatty substance found inside the heads of sperm whales. But even the best candles don't emit much light, and long before the French knew about wattage they knew, "By candlelight a goat is ladylike." Lanterns were only marginally better, and even when they appeared by decree outside European residences in the early fourteen-hundreds, they couldn't compete with a moonless night. Oil lamps, which were almost as ineffective, remained relatively unpopular until the eighteenth century, when technological innovations increased their brightness while minimizing the noxious fumes they released.

Better lamps and a demand for public lighting finally resulted in nearly five thousand oil lamps being installed in London in 1736. Ten years later, the prevalence of lamps in Paris led one Frenchman to declare, "The reign of the night is finally going to end." It didn't, of course, and when gas mantles were introduced in London in 1807, the *Times* breathlessly declared, "There is nothing so important to the British realm, since that of navigation." The writing was on the wall, and, since gas lamps were ten to twelve times brighter than oil lamps, you could see it. With gas lights replacing lanterns and oil lamps, and watchmen giving way to official police forces, private and public events were moved back, shops closed their doors later, coach companies added to their nighttime schedules, and manufacturing began to go on around the clock.

By the mid-seventeenth century, nights were not only less sinister, they were, Ekirch insists, fun: "in spite of myriad perils, it was night, not morning, not afternoon, that was valued most." This rather grand claim for the night's sudden appeal may have more to do with Ekirch's relief at no longer having to read about the terrors associated with the night than it does with ironclad evidence. Still, he's able to enlist a Welsh proverb that catches the sentiment nicely: John in the morning becomes Jack at night.

In general, Ekirch doesn't so much argue his case as let the facts speak for themselves. And it's not just what people did that draws his attention; anything even remotely associated with the night—fuels, wicks, torches, chimneys, curtains, weapons, superstitions—is tossed into the mix. Ekirch is like some trivia-mad guide who finds his own section of the universe unfailingly interesting, and quite often we do, too. Only a curmudgeonly reader would object to learning about "linkboys," candle-bearing escorts who accompanied timorous pedestrians around seventeenth-century London at night; or about "moon-men," who rode ahead of coaches or carriages holding a pole topped by a globular lantern.

Regrettably, however, Ekirch doesn't know when to hold back. Maybe it's mean to ask an author who has consulted twenty-one volumes of *The Statistical Account of Scotland: Drawn Up from the Communications of the Ministers of Different Parishes* to refrain from giving us the full fruits of his research, but, beyond a certain point, evidence no longer qualifies as knowledge. If a lot of accidents occurred after nightfall, a few examples will suffice; three robberies serve as well as thirteen to suggest the night's perils. Ekirch's catalogue of arson, drunkenness, and thievery would be justifiable if the quality of the crimes were shown to have changed radically over the centuries, but he seems more interested in the numbers. It's almost as if his immersion in the night has made everything gray. It's one thing to be told about the Ufficiali di Notte, a Florentine court convened after dark, whose docket included the prosecution of homosexuals, but do we actually require documentation that some men awoke with hangovers in 1700?

Nor does Ekirch shy from the obvious; at times, he fairly runs to embrace it. "Night was a fertile time for romantic liaisons of all sorts," he informs us, adding, "More than a few male suitors earned reputations for whispering false promises to young women." On the other hand, it's good to be reminded that servants frolicked at night and that slaves' spirits rose as the sun fell; and one can only be grateful to Ekirch for reporting a North Carolina planter's words about slaves' slant on time: "Night was their day."

Any book about the night would be incomplete without a word about sleep, and, about three-quarters of the way through this one, Ekirch steers us toward the land of Nod. A good night's sleep for people in pre-industrial society was, at best, a long shot. There may not have been car alarms, ambulance sirens, or pneumatic drills, but there were watchmen shouting, bells ringing, dogs howling, mice scampering, roofs leaking, timbers shrinking, and chamber pots smelling. Most people slept on straw pallets or rough mats, or perhaps shared a cot with two or three siblings, along with fleas, lice, and bugs. Chronic fatigue was the norm, and sleep was valued in ways that we probably can't imagine. What rouses us from our own dogmatic slumbers, however, is Ekirch's assertion that "until the close of the early modern era, Western Europeans on most evenings experienced two major intervals of sleep bridged by up to an hour or more of wakefulness." People, evidently, awoke after midnight and, instead of tossing and turning, they regularly got up to talk, study, pray, and do chores.

In case we're skeptical, Ekirch has found references to the "first sleep," or *primo somno*, and the second sleep, sometimes called "morning sleep," in literature and letters. He has dug up a medical text that advised people with digestive problems to fall asleep on their right side during "the fyrste slepe," and "after the fyrste slepe turne on the lefte side"; and he assures us that Plutarch, Livy, and Virgil all invoked the term. Indeed, Ekirch supplies enough corroboration regarding the first and second snoozes to make segmented sleep seem like one of those customs, such as bundling and dog-baiting, which simply disappeared. "That all men sleep by intervals" required no further elaboration from John Locke, who did much of his sleeping during the latter part of the seventeenth century. Two hundred or so years later, as Ekirch sees it, artificial light had become so prevalent that people's sleep patterns began to change. Those who lived in cities were now able to work, read, and play long after nightfall, and seg-mented sleep gradually disappeared from urban culture.

What evolved is a shorter, seamless sleep, which, on the face of it, doesn't sound that bad. But Ekirch views our trun-cated sleep not just as a neutral statistic of modern life but as an offense against nature. Not only do we get too little sleep; our increased exposure to luminosity has "altered circadian rhythms as old as man himself." This, rather dismayingly, turns out to have some support in the medical community. In a study conducted at the National Institute of Mental Health which re-created conditions of "prehistoric" sleep, Dr. Thomas Wehr deprived volunteers of artificial light for up to fourteen hours at night for a span of several weeks. As Ekirch notes, the "subjects first lay awake in bed for two hours, slept for four, awakened again for two or three hours of quiet rest and reflection, and fell back asleep for four hours before finally awakening for good." In short, they began to exhibit "a pattern of broken slumber —one practically identi-cal to that of pre-industrial households."

Wehr also observed that "the intervening period of 'non-anxious wakefulness' possessed 'an endocrinology all its own,' with visibly heightened levels of prolactin, a pituitary hormone best-known for stimulating lactation in nursing mothers and for permitting chickens to brood contentedly atop eggs for long stretches of time." And because Wehr "lik-ened this period of wakefulness to something approaching an altered state of consciousness not unlike meditation," Ekirch proposes that we have lost touch with that deeper, more pri-mal aspect of ourselves which emerges during moments after the first sleep. "By turning night into day," he writes, "mod-ern technology has helped to obstruct our oldest path to the human psyche." If Ekirch is correct, then Thomas Edison placed entirely too much faith in his lighting device. "Put an undeveloped human being into an environment where there is artificial light," Edison predicted, "and he will improve."

But will he sleep as nature intended? It's hard to say. Most scientists are confident that internal biological timers regulate body temperature, hormone production, and sleep levels; and they're pretty sure that the suprachiasmatic nucleus in the hypothalamus regulates circadian oscillations. The neurobiology of the sleep-wake cycle is not in dispute, but it's one thing to know that some psychotic episodes are linked to malfunctioning biological clocks, and quite another to assert that segmented sleep is essential to some deeper understanding of who we are.

On what, then, does Ekirch rest his argument? Simply this: Because the break in sleep occurs at the end of an R.E.M. cycle (when dreaming is frequent), our ancestors were better attuned to the part of the subconscious which is responsible for dreams. And because they customarily jotted down their impressions of dreams, it's clear that they took them more seriously than we do. By "they," Ekirch means the literate middle class, who supplied what evidence exists of segmented sleep. Apparently, the wealthy, who stayed up late, either enjoyed undivided sleep or failed to say otherwise. As for common laborers, they didn't know how to write, so there is scant evidence that they slept in shifts and none to suggest that, had they awakened around midnight, they would have mulled over their dreams. It seems far more likely that a peasant, having spent ten or twelve hours in the fields clearing rocks, probably slept like one.

It should be noted that Ekirch's conclusion about the origins, if not the inadequacies, of seamless sleep was in dispute even before the publication of his book. In "Caffeine and the Coming of the Enlightenment," a brisk, informative essay that appeared in a 2003 issue of *Raritan*, Roger Schmidt, an English professor at Idaho State, stands Ekirch's argument on its head. According to Schmidt, it was the introduction of caffeine and coffee houses in the late seventeenth century, along with the practice of late-night reading, the development of the first accurate clocks and timepieces, and the consolidation of the Protestant ethos ("Time is money"), that worked to devalue the idea of sleep. And this, in turn, "created a demand for better nocturnal lighting." Just what we need: another chicken-or-egg argument.

Never mind. Ekirch is a man on a mission and, to a remarkable degree, he has reclaimed that portion of the circadian cycle which historians have traditionally neglected. He has emptied night's pockets and laid the contents out before us. If the resulting work, with all its proverbs, adages, anecdotes, facts, and figures, smells a little of the lamp, it's a fair trade-off. *At Day's Close* serves to remind us of night's ancient mystery, of the real reason we reach for the light switch. Ultimately, it's not the wattage but Dante's *lustro sopra* that we yearn for— God's grandeur flaming out "like shining from shook foil." The night may also be His handiwork, but who really likes the dark except vampires and people with sensitive retinas? Darkness suggests ignorance and hopelessness, and, as a symbol of despair or bad tidings, it can't be beat. Would Sir Edward Grey, the British Foreign Secretary, be remembered half so well had he not mused, after seeing a lamp-lighter turning up the gas lamps outside his office on the eve of the First World War, "The lamps are going out all over Europe; we shall not see them lit again in our lifetime"? No one wants the lights to go out, and all our valiant attempts to illuminate the night are merely fearful expressions of the permanent darkness that awaits.

3

SLANG-WHANGER

William Hazlitt's Impetuous Prose

Prepare yourself: you cannot be both a Coleridgean and a Hazlittean. I'm sorry, but it needed to be said. This doesn't mean that you can't like both "Kubla Khan" and "The Indian Jugglers," but somewhere along the line you have to choose. It's an ontological thing. Coleridge had an idealizing nature, Hazlitt a skeptical one. Coleridge gravitated toward the Absolute; Hazlitt fled from it. Coleridge believed that poetry was generated by "severe laws of the intellect;" Hazlitt believed that it was forged in the crucible of the sympathetic imagination. Coleridge argued that opposites exist in order to be reconciled; Hazlitt couldn't reconcile himself to that—or to much else, for that matter.

Such differences, however, did not constitute a problem until 1983, when David Bromwich forced us to take sides with his unsurpassed study of Hazlitt's oeuvre? *Hazlitt: The Mind of a Critic*. In fact, until Bromwich came along, most students of literature didn't know there was an oeuvre. They might have read some of the better-known essays—"On Gusto" or "My First Acquaintance with Poets"—but how many had ever bothered to crack open P. P. Howe's 1930–1934 edition of Hazlitt's *Complete Works*, consisting of twenty-one volumes?

The truth is most people prefer Coleridge. Coleridge was a poet and did poetic things like smoke opium. He was also a critic and semi-philosopher, whose *Biographia Literaria* transformed literary criticism into a field of study distinct from literature itself. Hazlitt was also a critic and a self-styled metaphysician, but mostly he was seen as a working journalist and essayist, albeit one with such strong opinions that T. S. Eliot decided he was guilty of "crimes against taste."

It's only in the past couple of decades that Hazlitt has been enjoying a serious revival, mainly through the efforts of Michael Foot, the former leader of Britain's Labour party. Nearly four years ago, when he was ninety-two, Foot, who credits Hazlitt with giving to "the English Left a perspective and philosophy as widely ranging as Burke had given to the English Right," founded the Hazlitt Society, whose members include, among others, the poet Tom Paulin, the philosopher A. C. Grayling, and the literature professors Jon Cook, Uttara Natarajan, and Duncan Wu. These are not fair-weather Hazlitteans. They read one another's manuscripts, write prefaces and laudatory introductions to one another's books, and band together to edit Hazlitt's writings. Between 1998 and 2005, they accounted for two major biographies, four critical studies, a nine-volume edition of Hazlitt's writings, and three smaller editions. Two years ago, Jon Cook published *Hazlitt in Love* and Duncan Wu presented us with a two-volume set of Hazlitt's uncollected writings. Wu has now followed up with *William Hazlitt: The First Modern Man*, which, even more that its predecessors, argues for Hazlitt's cultural centrality.

Four things commend Hazlitt to his followers: his fierce radicalism, his sensitive and critical intelligence, his alternately sunny and sullen disposition, and his prose—his "vigorous," "versatile," "flexible," "slouchy," "layered," "sauntering," "cascading," "nervy," "sinewy," "textured" prose. For Tom Paulin, Hazlitt is nothing less than "the first great theatre critic in English, the first great art critic, a magnificent political journalist and polemicist." A. C. Grayling, showing restraint, calls him simply "the greatest prose writer of the age."

William Hazlitt was born in Maidstone, Kent, on April 10, 1778. His mother was the daughter of a dissenting ironmonger from Suffolk, and his father, the son of Irish Presbyterians, became a Unitarian minister. An outspoken advocate for social and political reform, the Reverend Hazlitt, after a five-year posting in America, was assigned to the village of Wem, in Shropshire, where it was thought he could do the least harm. Hoping that his son would follow him into the ministry, he sent him to the Unitarian New College, at Hackney, in London, where the fifteen-year-old Hazlitt encountered the political writings of Hume, Godwin, and Priestley. By his second year, he had forgotten about ordination and, much to the disappointment of his parents, left the college. He had decided to become a painter and a philosopher.

Hazlitt was still shuttling between London and his parents' house when, in 1798, Coleridge, himself a Unitarian minister, came to Shrewsbury to preach. Hazlitt walked the ten miles from Wem to hear him, and two days later Coleridge paid a call on the Reverend Hazlitt. The next morning, Coleridge invited the young Hazlitt to visit him in Somerset. Hazlitt then walked Coleridge six miles down the road, listening as the other man dilated on various philosophers, talking so rapidly that he appeared "to float in air, to slide on ice."

Hazlitt was exhilarated, and that winter all he could think was: "I was to visit Coleridge in the Spring."

When Hazlitt finally arrived in Somerset, Coleridge introduced him to Wordsworth, his collaborator on the *Lyrical Ballads*. Although Hazlitt was deeply impressed by Wordsworth, he felt closer to Coleridge. The two men were well matched; both were self-absorbed, but one loved to talk incessantly and the other liked to listen. Coleridge, in thrall to Kant and Schiller, expatiated on the relation between sensation, thought, and feeling; Hazlitt, a disciple of Hume, stressed the mental involutions that drive behavior. Coleridge seemed dazzled by the mind's intricate pattern, Hazlitt by the texture of its weave. Years later, Hazlitt wrote about Coleridge as though recalling a schoolboy crush: "He is the only person I ever knew who answered to the idea of a man of genius. He is the only person from whom I ever learnt anything . . . His voice rolled on the air like the pealing organ, and its sound alone was the music of thought."

After moving to London to study painting in 1799, Hazlitt was introduced into the literary circle of Charles Lamb and his sister Mary. He managed to obtain a few commissions (his portrait of Lamb is in the collection of the National Portrait Gallery), but he was slow and he didn't bother to prettify his subjects. In 1808, he married a friend of the Lambs, Sarah Stoddart, with whom he had a son. Too poor to live in London, they rented a house in Wiltshire, where Hazlitt painted and also began to write in earnest. Since portraiture wasn't paying the bills, and Sarah Hazlitt was getting testy, he took a job in 1812 as a parliamentary reporter for the *Morning Chronicle*. Before long, he was reviewing drama, poetry, operas, novels, and art exhibitions for the *Chronicle* and other magazines, and by the end of the decade he had become the most formidable critic of his day.

Hazlitt was probably the first critic to think hard about prose and the first to recognize that prose, no less than poetry, reflected a fundamental worldview. Just as Coleridge and Wordsworth's *Lyrical Ballads* had discarded the formality and cadence of the Augustan poets, so Hazlitt rejected the exact and measured language of Sir Thomas Browne and Samuel Johnson, fashioning a prose whose emotional and political intensity colored everything he wrote. In approaching the arts, he combined the coolness of a surgeon with the fervor of an adept. When operating on a poem, he made the blood flow just enough not to leave any drops on the floor. "He is so afraid of doing wrong . . . that he does little or nothing," Hazlitt said of Thomas Campbell. "He writes according to established etiquette. He offers the Muses no violence." And he *liked* Campbell's poetry. He also admired Shelley, but couldn't overlook his weakness for intellectual fads. "He tampers with all sorts of obnoxious subjects; but it is less because he is gratified with the rankness of the taint than captivated with the intellectual phosphoric light they emit . . . Still I could wish that he would put a stop to the incessant, alarming whirl of his voltaic battery. With his zeal, his talent, and his fancy, he would do more good and less harm if he were to give up his wilder theories, and if he took less pleasure in feeling his heart flutter in unison with the panic-struck apprehensions of his readers." And when discussing Shakespeare's *Coriolanus*, Hazlitt examined the nature of poetry itself:

> The language of poetry naturally falls in with the language of power . . . The principle of poetry is a very anti-leveling principle. It aims at effect, it exists by contrast. It admits of no medium. It is every thing by excess. It rises above the

ordinary standard of sufferings and crimes. It presents a dazzling appearance . . . Poetry is right-royal. It puts the individual for the species, the one above the infinite many, might before right. A lion hunting a flock of sheep or a herd of wild asses is a more poetical object than they; and we even take part with the lordly beast, because our vanity or some other feeling makes us disposed to place ourselves in the situation of the strongest party.

No one had written criticism quite like this before: it was learned yet lucid, informal yet persuasive; and its language, for all its elegance and poetic conceits, packed a subversive wallop. If Samuel Johnson was the more deliberate aphorist, Hazlitt was the more self-conscious literary architect. You quote lines from Johnson; you want to recite entire passages from Hazlitt. In time, the critic blossomed into the essayist who, as Johnson noted of another writer, "lets thoughts drop from his pen as they rise into his mind." Hazlitt seems to hold nothing back: thoughts, feelings, biases, and impressions flow from him in a stream of associative effusions. He seems, in fact, even more passionate that the poets he's examining. Perhaps that's why he wrote in prose; the pentameter would undoubtedly have constrained him.

But Hazlitt knew exactly what he was doing: he wished to combine the literary and the conversational into what he called the "familiar style." "Any one may mouth out a passage with a theatrical cadence or get upon stilts to tell his thoughts," he wrote. "But to write or speak with propriety and simplicity is a more difficult task." His style, however, is anything but simple. Hazlitt takes language for a ride. He doesn't keep it level and moving at one speed; he guns it, putting it through loops and dives and steep climbs. At the risk of offending Hazlitteans everywhere, it bears saying that his descriptive allusions, lengthy quotations, and rhetorical flourishes may in some cases obscure the solid thinking of the arguments. But it is precisely this lack of self-restraint, this willingness to expose himself, this passionate need to explore his own responses to the world that give his work its flare–like iridescences.

Hazlitt's range was impressive even by the non-specialized standards of the day. He wrote political pamphlets, abridged (at Coleridge's urging) Abraham Tucker's *The Light of Nature Pursued*, updated an English grammar, and began working on a history of English philosophy. He lectured on Shakespeare, Elizabethan literature, and the English comic writers; he gave us the concept of "gusto," which inspired Keats's idea of the chameleon poet; he wrote a biography of Napoleon; and he all but invented, if we don't count Plutarch, the profile of the contemporary celebrity. He was, in fact, the first of the great ambidextrous essayists, one hand thumping out politics and philosophy, the other executing glissandos of aesthetic appreciation.

Duncan Wu's claim that Hazlitt is "the first modern man," is, however, a stretch. Hazlitt may have possessed, as Wu states, "a new sensibility" and a psychological grasp of people's behavior, but the same can be said about Rousseau, Shakespeare, and Johnson. What's modern about Hazlitt, and specific to him, is his role as a journalist at a time when journalism, especially periodical journalism, was becoming a staple of British society. A hundred and fifty years before the New Journalists of the nineteen-sixties rubbed our noses in their egos, Hazlitt put himself into his work with a candor that would have been unthinkable a few generations earlier.

It was a good time to be a critic. Not only were there as many literary egotists flitting in and out of London as had ever been assembled at one time—Wordsworth, Coleridge, Southey, Leigh Hunt, Byron, Shelley, Keats, Lamb, de Quincey—but dozens of magazines were being launched that proved instrumental in furthering the careers of both poets and journalists. Unlike their eighteenth-century forerunners— *The Tatler, The Spectator, The Gentleman's Magazine*—the periodicals hatching around the time of the Regency (1811–20) specialized in making criticism a spectator sport.

According to the British literary scholar Bonamy Dobrée, men of letters in the mid-eighteenth century prided themselves on writing in a "middle style" that reflected the "voice of society" (a bolder style would have constituted an offense against taste). But, of course, these men were writing for a society that consisted basically of themselves. When Hazlitt turned to journalism, there was a larger audience ready and willing to buy books, and it wanted news about literature in words that it could understand. The periodicals, which encouraged their contributors to write in idiomatic, straight shooting prose, thus helped make literature sociable. The pedant gave way to the polemicist, the Critick to the critic-reviewer, and culture became a topic of public discussion—and dissension.

In fact, literary journalism, in its first incarnation, was probably as intense as it would ever become. This was a period when the monarchy was teetering, banks were failing, taxes were onerous, unemployment was high, and the upper classes were fretting about Jacobins and revolutionaries. Conservatism was equated with repression, radicalism with sexual libertinism. Tory magazines such as *Blackwood's, John Bull,* and the *Quarterly Review* castigated republicans; Whiggish periodicals such as the *Morning Chronicle*, *The Edinburgh Review*, and *The London Magazine* reprimanded anyone holding Royalist views.

Apart from the small matter that Hazlitt lived in and around London during the first quarter of the nineteenth century, he could have been a New York intellectual of the Sixties, involved in the same kind of infighting, shifting alliances, gossiping, and name-calling. Hazlitt, an avowed republican, was labeled "an infidel, a Jacobin, and a whoremonger" and dismissed as a "Cockney Aristotle"—i.e., a lower-class writer who wanted to sound like his betters. In August, 1818, *Blackwood's* published such an outrageous attack that Hazlitt sued for libel and eventually accepted an out-of-court settlement. To his critics he would always be "a slang-whanger" who wished "to destroy the very foundations of modesty and decorum." According to Duncan Wu, "No writer was more reviled, and none were less deserving of it."

Hazlitt may not have deserved the abuse, but he certainly asked for it. The man suffered from intellectual Tourette's syndrome: he simply could not keep his mouth shut. Hazlitt saw a violation and immediately wrote out a ticket, and nothing you could say or do would make him reconsider. He couldn't even stop himself from biting the hand of Francis Jeffrey, whose magazine, *The Edinburgh Review*, helped feed him. If there was something honorable about this, there was also something cold. After finishing a not altogether favorable profile of Byron, Hazlitt learned that the poet had recently died. He could have revised, but he chose not to, explaining that it would be wrong to "turn undertakers' men to fix the glittering plate upon the coffin, or fall into the procession of popular woe. Death cancels everything but truth."

Naturally, there were consequences. He alienated Coleridge, Southey, and Wordsworth, whose political changes of heart deeply disappointed him. Hazlitt, who never wavered in his good opinion of the French Revolution and persisted in his admiration for Napoleon even when France and England were at war, was incensed by the backsliding of those who renounced their radicalism. Although he and Coleridge remained on speaking terms for fifteen years and found themselves living next door to one another in 1811 (Hazlitt's wife had booted him out of the house), the friendship gradually soured. And, in 1816, when Coleridge published *The Statesman's Manual*, which urged political reform based on Scripture, Hazlitt exploded: "Everlasting inconsequentiality marks all he does".

Hazlitt may have been tightly wound and easily hurt, but he could inflict hurt in return. Those who blasted him in print knew they were cocking a weapon that could shoot straighter than their own standard-issue prose. He reserved his deepest scorn, of which he had a plentiful supply, for those who esteemed authority over independence. "The love of liberty is the love of others," Hazlitt asserted, "the love of power is the love of ourselves."

> I am no politician, and less still can I be said to be a party-man: but I have a hatred of tyranny, and a contempt for its tools; and this feeling I have expressed as often and as strongly as I could. I cannot sit quietly down under the claims of barefaced power, and I have tried to expose the little arts of sophistry by which they are defended. I have no mind to have my person made a property of, nor my understanding made a dupe of. I deny that liberty and slavery are convertible terms, that right and wrong, truth

and falsehood, plenty and famine, the comforts or wretch-
edness of a people, are matters of perfect indifference. That
is all I know of the matter.

In his essay "The Fight," Hazlitt recalls overhearing one
man say to another, "Confound it, man, don't be insipid," and
thinking, "that's a good phrase." Certainly no one could
accuse *him* of insipidness. All that he felt, he felt intensely.
Gusto, or experience felt *vividly*, marked everything he did,
and he came by it both physiologically and literally. He appro-
priated the Latin ablative *gustus*, meaning "to taste," lopped
off two letters, added the "o," infused it with then current
notions of taste, sympathy, and imagination, and, presto, a
new concept was born. More complicated than how we think
of it today, gusto was nicely summed up by Timothy Corrigan
as "objectively experiencing the expressive vividness of a
world eliciting our disinterested sympathy." Hazlitt put it
another way: "Those who have the largest hearts, have the
soundest understandings."

There are writers who hide behind their words and there are
those who shoulder up beside you. Hazlitt's "essays are
emphatically himself," Virginia Woolf observed. "So thin is
the veil of the essay as Hazlitt wore it, his very look comes
before us." True, we feel that we know the writer, but how
well do we know the man who doesn't write, the one who
gets his hair cut, who knocks back a warm beer with friends?
The fact is, essayists lie. They may not mean to, but they do.
Like all writers, they create effects by adopting a tone, a
tempo, a manner of address. Hazlitt's breezy, self-confident
style gives the impression of a man secure enough to admit
his own failings. Even when he regards himself in a quizzical

light—a man who causes women to "split their sides with laughing at him"—we chalk it up to literary brio. We don't for a moment believe that he's inept, or unattractive, or capable of behaving like a lunatic. You can't write well and behave badly.

But, of course, you can, and Hazlitt did. He cheated on his wife, fought with friends and acquaintances, and when Napoleon was defeated at Waterloo he stayed drunk for weeks. For all the insouciance of his prose, Hazlitt could be a social disaster. His friend P. G. Patmore said that he entered a room "as if he had been brought back to it in custody." Coleridge famously described him as "brow-hanging, shoe-contemplative, strange." He was obviously combative, but, according to Wu, he was afraid of his housekeeper. He could stare down publishers, but was reluctant on a cold night to ask a stranger to shut the window of a coach. Perhaps that's one reason that bookish people are drawn to Hazlitt: he's terribly self-conscious in public and acutely conscious of the self in private; like them, he gets buffeted by fate or by people with more power, but unlike them, he buffets back, which makes him, well, heroic.

Every essay should be regarded as a self-portrait of the author at his or her desk, not in the world. The new Hazlitteans, however, tend to see their man as he wants to be seen. Stanley Jones, who wrote a fine biography of Hazlitt in 1989, practically wrung his hands at the thought of Hazlitt's venturing into the cut-throat literary world of London. It's Hazlitt, though, who creates the impression that he wasn't made for the rough and tumble, that he was better suited for the purely contemplative life—a Regency Thomas Merton minus the Cross. It's an appealing picture, but it's incomplete. Hazlitt was an ambitious, tough-minded, and tireless self-promoter with a physicality that biographers like Wu are only now picking up on. He walked, boxed, and played fives (an early form of racquetball), and "his sighs, groans, lamentations left no doubt that he was becoming warm in the spirit of the game." Patmore recalls seeing him, McEnroe-like, "fling his racket to the other end of the court, walk deliberately to the centre, with uplifted hands imprecate the most fearful curses on his head for his stupidity, and then rush to the side wall and literally dash his head against it." Nor did Hazlitt's combustible personality temper with age. The editor Robert Bell, who met him later in life, remarked, "There was not a particle of energy about him ordinarily . . . But when he kindled, a flush spread over his sunken cheeks, his eyes lighted up wildly, his chest expanded, he looked like one inspired, his motions were eloquent, and his whole form partook of the enthusiasm."

Hazlitt kindled in more ways than one. Although he intimated that Petrarch's unconsummated love for Laura was perfection, since "that which exists in the imagination is alone imperishable," Hazlitt consummated to a degree that even his friends felt was excessive. The truth is he was a nincompoop when it came to women. This needs saying because of two episodes in his life, both of which did irreparable harm to his reputation; the first because of lies spread by Coleridge and Wordsworth, the second because of his own propensity to tell the truth.

In 1803, while visiting Coleridge in the Lake District, Hazlitt chatted up a local woman in a tavern in Keswick. Either she insulted him or she rejected his advances, and he, so the story goes, lifted up her skirts and spanked her. When a party of her friends came around to give Hazlitt a ducking in a nearby pond, Coleridge packed him off to Wordsworth's house, in Grasmere. In Coleridge's later accounts of the mishap, he saved Hazlitt's life from two hundred mounted villagers, and, over the years, as relations between the men worsened, Coleridge and Wordsworth spitefully embroidered on the story, playing up Hazlitt's addiction "to women, as objects of sexual indulgence."

The next incident had nothing at all comical about it. In the summer of 1820, Hazlitt, now formally separated from his wife, took lodgings in Camden, London, and promptly fell in love with the landlord's daughter Sarah Walker. Hazlitt was forty-two, Sarah nineteen. It's difficult to know how much she encouraged him, as we have only Hazlitt's word for these events, but her telling him at one point "I always told you I had no affection for you" should have been a clue. Nonetheless, for two years Hazlitt thought about her constantly, finding hope in her smallest gesture. Staking everything on a few caresses she had allowed him, Hazlitt divorced his wife—a complicated procedure that required both of them to establish residency in Scotland—and threw himself at Sarah's feet. But when he returned from Scotland he found her with another man.

"I cannot forget her, and I can find no other like what she seemed," Hazlitt said. So he did what writers do: he wrote a book—in this case, an odd duck of a book, titled *Liber Amoris; or, The New Pygmalion*. It purports to be the papers of a man recently deceased in the Netherlands and consists of a number of quick scenes and conversations between "H" and "S," followed by a series of letters that the anonymous author wrote and received while in Scotland. Many of the letters were real; a few were composed solely for the book itself. As usual, Hazlitt holds nothing back. He describes his obsession unsparingly, omitting no embarrassing detail, including his fear that the girl "runs mad for size."

Hazlitt must have known that his authorship would be discovered. He had made no secret of the "affair" and didn't hide the fact that he was writing about it. He hoped that doing so would be cathartic, but the only thing *Liber Amoris* seems to have accomplished was to give his enemies another stick to beat him with. A month after its publication, in 1823, the periodical *John Bull*, which had got hold of one of Hazlitt's letters to Sarah Walker, gleefully printed it, removing the book's fig leaf of fiction,—and the bloodletting began: "a disgusting mass of profligacy and dullness," one critic wrote; the result of "a cockney's stupidity and folly," said another. The most galling review, however, might have been the one from the friendly critic who maintained that Hazlitt could not be the author, since only a fool could have written such a book. Hazlitt's reputation never recovered. He wrote some of his best essays after 1823, but his books, which had never sold well, now barely sold at all.

Hazlitt did finally manage to put the girl behind him, and, in 1824, he married again. His new wife had a little money, but didn't seem inclined to spend it all on Hazlitt, and after they toured France and Italy she remained in Switzerland while he tried to make ends meet in London— never an easy thing for him to do. Despite writing millions of words during his career, Hazlitt barely scratched out a living. He was hounded by creditors, chased by bailiffs, and even jailed briefly in February, 1823. During one such low point, Wu claims, without evidence, Keats dropped in on Hazlitt to discuss his own prospects as a reviewer and journalist. He found him sitting alone in a bare room, having recently sold his furniture and paintings to pay off his debts. Keats stuck to poetry.

Wu's book, despite its defensive attitude and some unfortu-nate phrasings (his moods "went up and down like a yo-yo"; "She had a lot going for her"), is fun to read. Coleridge, Wordsworth, Lamb, and Leigh Hunt slide in and out of the narrative, sniping, complaining, gossiping, but, most of all, *thinking*. If Wu errs, it's on the side of enthusiasm. He doesn't even feign disinterest. None of the new Hazlitteans do. Only rarely does one of them allow that their man may have been too prickly, too tough on his friends, too indifferent to his wives. Wu sticks up for Hazlitt at almost every turn, finding a reason to justify nearly everything he said and did. Even the outrageous is carefully reconfigured as normalcy. Hazlitt once brought a prostitute to his rooms when his ten-year-old son William was visiting. Understandably upset, the boy told his mother, who then gave Hazlitt an earful. Instead of letting this go, Wu asks us to remember that "childhood as we know it is a Victorian construct, and Hazlitt wanted William (how-ever misguidedly) to learn the ways of the world under his supervision rather than alone, or with school friends." If that's the case, why did Sarah Hazlitt, sixteen years before Victoria ascended to the throne, get so worked up? Victorian scruples aside, couldn't Hazlitt at least have waited until the boy was bar-mitzvahed?

"Well, I've had a happy life," Hazlitt remarked, on his deathbed. "It was what he would have said," Stanley Jones concludes. Grayling and Wu concur. But it's hard to resist shouting "Wrong!" By no stretch of the imagination did Hazlitt have a happy life. Seven years earlier, thinking of Sarah Walker, he had written, "I have wanted only one thing to make me happy; but wanting that have wanted every-thing!" Frankly, that, too, seems an exaggeration. No doubt both statements were heartfelt, but that doesn't make them accurate. His biographers, taking him at his word, emphasize his resoluteness and consistency. But Hazlitt had his moods; he was human, and he changed his mind. "As to my old opinions, I am heartily sick of them," he complained in the winter of 1823:

> They have deceived me sadly. I was taught to think, and I was willing to believe, that genius was not a bawd, that virtue was not a mask, that liberty was not a name, that love had its seat in the human heart. Now I would care little if these words were struck out of the dictionary, or if I had never heard them.

However, in one of his last essays, "The Letter-Bell," he's back to his old self: "I have never given the lie to my own soul. If I have felt any impression once, I feel it more strongly a second time; and I have no wish to revile and discard my best thoughts." Once again, and for the last time, he brings up Coleridge and can't resist getting in a few more digs. The mixture of sadness and resentment he feels so many years later only testifies to the warmth of that first friendship. He consoles himself with an old refrain: "There is at least a thorough *keeping* in what I write—not a line that betrays a principle or disguises a feeling. If my wealth is small, it all goes to enrich that same heap; and trifles in this way accumulate to a tolerable sum."

He died, owing money, in a cheap rooming house on Frith Street on September 18, 1830. His landlady is said to have hidden the body under the bed while she showed the room. The building has since been converted into a small hotel. It has thirty bedrooms, with antique furniture, claw-footed freestanding baths, and old-fashioned pull-chain cisterns. It's called Hazlitt's. Coleridgeans are welcome.

4

TOO TRUE

The Art of the Aphorism

There is something faintly comical in devoting a large number of words to the aphorism, which by consensus is a short, independent statement with a bite to it. At the same time, there is also something both clarifying and bracing in thinking about the subject, because what seems self-evident turns out to be anything but. For one thing, where does the adage end and the aphorism begin? Is an aphorism a proverb in stylish dress? An epigram with an extra layer? An axiom, only less rigorous? "Maxim" comes closest, I think, in general conversation to the aphorism, though few aphorisms have the thudding finality of most maxims. A successful aphorism provokes; it makes us think. Then again, it could be so forcefully, so pungently stated that deeper reflection seems unnecessary. Nonetheless, aphorisms *are* brief and, therefore, quotable.

But, no, not even that. Nietzsche, one of the best practitioners of the form, applied the term to prose passages of various lengths (only his most dedicated readers can quote them in full); and Kafka, the master of the parable, also, as it turns out, wrote aphorisms that often overshot the mark. Kafka's aphorisms came to light, in 2004, with the publication of *The Zürau Aphorisms*, which consists of numbered fragments, many with a theological theme. They were discovered by Roberto Calasso in the Bodleian Library and seem to have been composed while Kafka was recuperating from tuberculosis at his sister's home in Zürau between 1917 and 1918. Each fragment unfurls on a separate slip of onionskin paper and, according to Calasso's afterword, is an aphorism only "in the Kierkegaardian sense [of] an 'isolated' entity, which must be surrounded by an empty space in order to breathe." In fact, only a few have the brio of a recognizable aphorism: "Goodness is in a certain sense comfortless." The fragments explore rather than stake a claim; instead of sounding like a riposte or a retort, a discriminating judgment succinctly presented (like Kafka's own oft-quoted and unZürau-like "A book must be the axe for the frozen sea within us"), they are content to stir the water rather than dunk our heads in it.

"Aphorism," from the Greek *aphorismos*, is literally a distinction or a definition; and models—snatches of song or superstition—probably existed long before anyone thought to give them a name. The first aphorisms most likely dealt with religion and rules of behavior and were handed down from generation to generation, changing as the culture changed. Hippocrates (c. 460–c. 375 B.C.) is usually considered the first published aphorist, and the opening six words of his famous book on medicine may sound familiar: "Life is short, and art long; the crisis fleeting; experience perilous; and decision difficult."

If Hollywood were all we had to go by, arms and orgies preoccupied the ancient Greeks and Romans. The truth is somewhat less exciting. When media consisted of vocal cords and styluses, the better you spoke, the higher you rose; and the words that found their way into everyday discourse were the epigrammatic statements of men who spoke in public.[1] (What is a statesman except someone who makes public statements?) Consequently, rhetoric—one of the three original liberal arts (the other two being grammar and dialectic)— amounted to verbal persuasion. In the *Rhetorica ad Herennium*, believed to be the oldest surviving Latin book on rhetoric, we read: "It is best we insert maxims discreetly, that we may be viewed as judicial advocates, not moral instructors."

According to the classicist Patrick Sinclair, the maxim or aphorism proper arose from *sententia*, a rhetorical device directly related to reading and citation. *Sententia* translates as "judgment" or "opinion;" and "sententious" originally did not have the connotation of pompous moralizing but referred to the impressions conveyed by reading Greek and Latin texts. It's not always clear which passages by Hesiod, Thales, Herodotus, Thucydides, Seneca, Cicero, Horace, Juvenal, Ovid, Lucretius, and Marcus Aurelius were intended as maxims and which became maxims because they were singled out by later writers; what is clear is that the ancient writers knew as much as we do about the vagaries of the human heart.

Human nature may be mercurial, but nature itself, according to Church doctrine, was stable and eternal. The old aphorisms about the cosmos were adequate to the task of defining it. But as the Middle Ages evolved into the Renaissance, the cosmos and man's place in it began to be viewed differently. Humanist philology and scientific skepticism gave rise to the modern essay and to writers for whom the "new Philosophie," ushered in by Copernicus and Kepler,"calls all in doubt." New philosophy meant new ways of acquiring and

---

[1] Martial (Marcus Valerius Martialis) created the epigram proper around 86 A.D. in the form of elegiac couplets.

storing knowledge, and along with an increase in plays, broadsides, books, sermons, and treatises, there emerged—when paper became cheap and plentiful—the private or commonplace book. Cobbled together by literate people, commonplace books served as repositories for whatever someone thought fit to record: medical recipes, jokes, verse, prayers, mathematical tables, aphorisms, and especially passages from letters, poems, or books. Ben Johnson kept one; so did John Milton, John Locke, and Thomas Jefferson. In fact, one might think that most writers would have fashioned such handy compendia, yet Shakespeare's has never been found.

Musing on the act of making such books, Robert Darnton notes that whenever one of these private bookmakers copied something into a notebook, he would do so "under an appropriate heading, adding observations made in the course of daily life." In effect, the "author" was creating aphorisms by designating passages worthy of inclusion. Darnton also tells us that "early modern Englishmen read in fits and starts and jumped from book to book. They broke texts into fragments and assembled them into new patterns by transcribing them in different sections of their notebooks. Then they reread the copies and rearranged the patterns while adding more excerpts." This segmented rather than sequential mode of reading, which prevailed until people started consuming novels, "compelled its practitioners to read actively . . . to impose their own pattern on their reading matter . . . Reading and writing were therefore inseparable activities."[2]

---

[2] Not many commonplace books get published these days. My own library includes *The Practical Cogitator* ("this anthology for the thinker") and W.H Auden's *A Certain World*. Of course, anyone can keep a commonplace book, and thousands of bloggers do, though one has to wonder whether it is knowledge that is being served or merely thousands of egos.

A segmented or aphoristic mode of thinking certainly characterizes philosopher and statesman Francis Bacon (1561–1626). Bacon not only kept a commonplace book, but some of his published works—*Apothegms* (1624) and *Essays* (1625)—have the feel of commonplace ones. Intrigued by the new mode of scientific thinking, Bacon decided there were two ways of getting at the truth: methodical investigation, which produced orderly and related data, and ordinary experience, which culminated in discrete, unsystematic judgments, or aphorisms. Far from being untrue, aphorisms "except they should be ridiculous . . . contain some good quantity of observation." Such observation "representing a knowledge broken, [does] invite men to inquire further; whereas Methods, carrying the show of a total, do secure men, as if they were at furthest."

Bacon's own aphorisms nicely embody his philosophical outlook: "If a man will begin with certainties, he shall end in doubts; but if he will be content to begin with doubts he shall end in certainties." The Enlightenment—the bringing of truth to light—was a good time for aphorists: with one fell syntactic swoop they could describe both nature and society, stripping away pretensions while rendering unfavorable verdicts on humanity. Francois duc de La Rochefoucauld (1613–1680), set the tone and perhaps the standard for the ruthlessly honest aphorist: "We all have strength enough to endure the misfortune of others," he wrote. "We often forgive those who bore us, but we cannot forgive those whom we bore." And (have at you, Donald Trump): "It takes greater character to carry off good fortune than bad."

In seventeenth-century France and to some extent in England, the making of maxims was a diversion of the salon crowd. Coining a witty epigram won you points, and if your lineage was suspect it helped if you could amuse your betters.

Many salons and hunting parties probably had their own versions of Truman Capote or Fran Liebowitz, wags who paid their way by throwing around knowing quips and delicious asides. Of course, once you gained a reputation as a wit, the pressure could be enormous. Quick and clever as these aphorism-spouting folks were, I suspect they awoke every morning and began devising the quotable sayings they could drop spontaneously at the dinner table.

Taking their cue and license from La Rochefoucauld's popular *Book of Maxims* (1665), the Marquis de Vauvenargues (1715–1747), Voltaire (1694–1778), Nicolas Chamfort (1741–1794), and Joseph Joubert (1754–1824) all issued collections of aphorisms. In Germany, Georg Lichtenberg (1742–1799) and, on occasion, Arthur Schopenhauer (1788–1860) were attracted to the form, which became no less popular in England and America. Benjamin Franklin, of course, produced his share, as did Alexander Pope (in rhyming couplets), and William Blake (in rhyming strangeness). Lords Chesterfield and Halifax were famous for their terse pronouncements, and Dr. Johnson went so far as to claim that "mankind may come, in time, to write all aphoristically except in narrative."

Not that all aphorisms were instantly admired and repeated, or, if repeated, permanently admired. What may have started out as a trenchant aphorism could, after much repetition, become a dullish proverb—perhaps the reason that Lord Chesterfield advised his son, "A man of fashion never has recourse to proverbs and vulgar aphorisms."[3] According to John Gross, whose *Oxford Book of Aphorisms* (1983) continues to be the best anthology of its kind, once the

---

[3] Today, some experts in the field of paremiology (the study of proverbs, as if you didn't know) argue that common expressions were largely dropped from polite speech in eighteenth-century England.

aphorism came "to denote the formulation of a moral or philosophical principle," it became possible for someone like the versifier Sir Richard Blackmore to dismiss Hippocrates' short work as a "book of jests." Although the word "aphorism" temporarily fell from grace, there is no reason to think that the dry witticism, sly put-down, or acute remark fell with it.

In any event, the word was resuscitated by Dr. Johnson, who included it in his *Dictionary*, and later it was given another boost by John Stuart Mill's 1837 review of a book of aphorisms called *Thoughts in the Cloister and the Crowd*. Mill picked up where Bacon had left off, or, to be uncharitable, simply picked up Bacon's notion that aphorisms were not, in Mill's words, the product of "long chains of reasoning" but rather were "exhibited in the same unconnected state in which they were discovered." Mill, who was a moral and political philosopher rather than a metaphysical one, liked the aphorism for its ability to sum up and deliver worldly truths, but his fondness for the form was nothing alongside Nietzsche's aspirations for it. With typical self-effacement, Nietzsche informs us that "The aphorism, the apophthegm, in which I am the first master among Germans, are the forms of 'eternity'; my ambition is to say in ten sentences what everyone else says in a book—what everyone else *does not* say in a book."

Nietzsche's early philological training, his aversion to transcendental screeds, and his reliance on impassioned language (whose tempo and shimmering intensity, he hoped, would create a psychological and pedagogical revolution) naturally drew him to the aphorism. He wanted not merely to explain the world but to expose received opinion for the debilitating sham that it was; he wanted, in effect, to rewire ways of thinking. And when we think of Nietzsche's own style, we may recall that the full title of *Twilight of the Idols* contains the phrase *Or How One Philosophizes with a Hammer*. Nietzsche added those words and the preface after the book was written and noted that the idols in question were "touched with a hammer as with a tuning fork." Less interested in smashing old ideas than in making new ones resonate, he insisted his style be both pellucid and powerful.

Most thinkers, Nietzsche maintained, "write badly because they communicate to us not only their thoughts but also the thinking of their thoughts." So if one wanted readers to think better, one had to write better. Nietzsche described his own writings as "fishhooks" intended to capture the reader's attention and presumably lift him from the murky metaphysical waters of Western thought. Aphorisms, of course, were the hook and the bait:

> The relief-like, incomplete presentation of an idea, of a whole philosophy, is sometimes more effective than its exhaustive realization: more is left for the beholder to do, he is more impelled to continue working on that which appears before him so strongly etched in light and shadow, to think it through to the end, and to overcome even that constraint which has hitherto prevented it from stepping forth fully formed.

Nietzsche, who preferred gods who philosophize to a God whose knowledge was absolute, would probably have regarded the coming of Ludwig Wittgenstein with a certain approval. Whatever one thinks of Wittgenstein's thought or the reversal of his thought, few would contend that he subscribed to a traditional presentation of ideas. Like Nietzsche, Wittgenstein wrote aphoristically, but not so much to forge a style as to express the ambiguity inherent in any description of reality. The problem with reality is that it keeps happening, and "Philosophy is therefore no theory, something with dogmas . . . it is an activity."

Philosophers may have written more about the aphorism than other writers, but it's not necessarily the deepest thinkers who come up with the most vivid examples. For one thing, philosophers have more on their minds than our foibles and follies. Those barbed formulations that uncover our pretensions and mock our self-regard are the product of native wit and social acumen. Aphorists—the good ones, at any rate—have irony in their souls. They may condemn the insincerity, stupidity, greed, and treachery of human beings, but instead of railing to high heaven they retaliate by rendering the perfectly phrased judgment. "Art is what you can get away with," quipped Andy Warhol. For those with experience of the art world, it was as if the cheap mechanism behind a complicated illusion had suddenly been revealed. And that's what the best aphorisms do: they point to a truth just out of range. Don't we realize almost immediately, though we've never said it aloud, that "The recipe for boredom is—completeness"? And because irony is not averse to paradox, a good aphorism can sometimes mock its own seriousness even while making a telling point: "If the rich could hire other people to die for them, the poor could make a wonderful living."

James Geary, author of *The World in a Phrase: A Brief History of the Aphorism* (2005) and *Geary's Guide to the World's Great Aphorists* (2007), claims that "Aphorisms give us the world in a phrase." Hardly. Some of them may proffer *a* world, but only when they link, as Mark Twain put it, and as

Geary reminds us, "a minimum of sound to a maximum of sense." It was Mill who pointed out that "any proposition epigrammatically expressed—almost always goes more or less beyond the strict truth." But it was the Viennese man-about-town Karl Kraus who said it aphoristically: "An aphorism never coincides with the truth: it is either a half-truth or one-and-a-half truths." This, of course, leads to the question of degree in Kraus's own definition: is his aphorism less than the truth or more? If you can parse this, you'll have no trouble deciding whether Thomas Macaulay's maxim that "Nothing is so useless as a general maxim" contradicts itself.

For W. H. Auden, who published a commonplace book in 1970, aphorisms "are essentially an aristocratic genre of writing. The aphorist does not argue or explain, he asserts, and implicit in his assertion is a conviction that he is wiser or more intelligent than his readers." Susan Sontag said much the same thing in describing the work of Roland Barthes: "It is in the nature of aphoristic thinking to be always in a state of concluding; a bid to have the final word is inherent in all powerful phrase-making." That final word is precisely what we want: a little bit of authority that we transform into certainty. Aphorisms often provide it—but at what cost?

Language does not merely express thought; it is the mold that forms thinking. Nietzsche knew this better than anyone and hoped that aphorisms would educate not by example but by inspiration. Aphorisms would reveal a door to knowledge we didn't know existed. The problem is that they may distract us from other openings, other doors of perception, as Blake might say. Those impressive autonomous statements, delivered in the guise of concentrated knowledge, can sometimes be *too* effective. Taken to heart, they have a way of shutting down the mind: "In spite of his practical ability," George Eliot said of the rector in *Daniel Deronda*, "some of his experience had petrified into maxims and quotations."

Milton admired elegant maxims but distrusted "tyrannous aphorisms," which, along with flattery and shifts in power, may instill "barren hearts with a conscientious slavery." A slavish adherence to the simplistic proposition is, in fact, the ethos of George Orwell's Ministry of Truth, whose slogans—WAR IS PEACE, FREEDOM IS SLAVERY, IGNORANCE IS STRENGTH—are verbal cudgels, intent on bending our will to the will of the state. The point is, when we abuse language, perverting agreed-upon meanings, we end up debasing ourselves. ARBEIT MACHT FREI is not itself a terrible or even false statement, but when placed above the gate leading to Auschwitz the words smolder with an irony that is nothing short of evil.

Anything that can educate can also manipulate, and anyone selling anything to the public—dictators, CEOs, advertising executives—knows the power of easy-to-remember expressions. I, for one, still believe that "It takes a tough man to make a tender chicken." Effective ad copy, of course, doesn't have to be true; it simply has to be catchy. But a well-honed aphorism not only stops us in our tracks; it impedes our moving forward. Even if we don't immediately buy into it, it can still deliver a wallop: "There is no female Mozart because there is no female Jack the Ripper," Camille Paglia tells us. Is this worth discussing? Or are we being bamboozled by the phrase's conspicuous symmetry? True or not, some aphorisms make it hard to imagine anything better ever being said on the subject: "Every class is unfit to rule," pronounced Lord Acton. "No snowflake in an avalanche ever feels responsible," observed Stanislaw Lec. *"Maximiste, pessimiste,"* concluded Joseph Roux.

And herein lies the danger as well as the appeal of the aphorism. A statement can be so well put that its cogency is entirely dependent on its formulation, but as soon as we reflect on it we may come to another conclusion. "If you are afraid of loneliness, do not marry," cautioned Chekhov. "In war, as in prostitution, amateurs are often better than professionals," declared Napoleon. Both statements untrue, I think. On the other hand, a little reflection may enhance the meaning of an aphorism. "Whatever his merits, a man in good health is always disappointing." For a second, this sounds merely provocative, but perhaps E. M. Cioran was talking about men so physically and mentally sound that they take life's vicissitudes in stride, displaying a bonhomie or steadfastness that, however admirable, is in the end simply boring.

Nietzsche's aphorism that "Every philosophy is the philosophy of some stage in life" suggests that our liking for specific aphorisms may very well change over time. Some statements become true only when experience catches up with them. A friend of mine who taught a college course in the aphorism used Bertrand de Fontenelle's line "I hate `war: it ruins conversation" as an example of the ironist's art. One of his students, however, quickly disagreed. She took the statement to be neither ironic nor witty, but factual. She had grown up in Kosovo during the Bosnian war and related that all conversation (except about the war) had stopped when the Serbs and the Croats began fighting.

It's impossible, in fact, to know which aphorisms people will find impressive. Paul Valéry's remark that "between men there are only two relations: logic or war" gave me a jolt when I first read it, but others may find it literally unremarkable. Indeed, the telling phrase that we commit to memory says more about ourselves, about our taste in books and people, than about anything else. Geary, for example, admires the installation art of Jenny Holzer, which utilizes sayings that she aptly calls "Truisms." I can't tell you why exactly Holzer's work leaves me cold, or why the folks at the *New York Times*, the Whitney Museum, and the Venice Biennale think otherwise, but I can tell you that her aphorisms—which are obviously parodistic, a critique of contemporary mores—do not make me reevaluate anything: "You are a victim of the rules you live by"; "Enjoy yourself because you can't change things anyway"; "Playing it safe can cause a lot of damage in the long run." After one acknowledges the platitudes' self-conscious irony—radiating from light-emitting diodes in museums, art galleries, and public places—what's left to know? What's left to think about?

Aphorisms have been described as meteorites, gunshots, lightning bolts, magic tricks, and particle accelerators. Derrida, in *Fifty-Two Aphorisms for a Foreword*, takes pains to inform us what the aphorism is not: "[It] is neither a house nor a temple, nor a school, nor a parliament, nor an agora, nor a tomb. Neither a pyramid, nor, above all, a stadium." Why?—you may ask. Because, as Derrida explains, "there is no inhabitable place for the aphorism." This strikes me as a fancy way of saying that the aphorism is difficult to confine and has a life apart from the life of its creator, but it doesn't really illustrate what makes the aphorism so appealing. Not every one of Derrida's fifty-two aphorisms deals with the aphorism, but those that do are philosophically arched: "12. This is an aphorism, he says. People will be content simply to cite it." "21. This is not an aphorism." (12, 21? Coincidence?) Number 46 seems to have caught the eye of a few critics: "Despite their fragmentary appearance, [aphorisms] make a sign toward the memory of totality, at the same time ruin and monument."

If Friedrich Hölderlin's assertion that "There is only one quarrel in the world: which is more important, the whole or the individual part?" has any merit, then Derrida's aphorism has some as well. Aphorisms *are* complete unto themselves, encapsulating the cultures that created them (which now have disappeared), and yet they are also incipient fragments, perhaps only slightly less transitory than the men who articulated them. But then one thinks, *everything* is a fragment of a greater whole, as well as, potentially, a ruin—you, me, the planet, the galaxy—and it becomes clear that the poignancy and seeming profundity of Derrida's statement rests more on the poetic juxtaposition of particular words than on any great truth.

Philosophers wrestle with words to make sense of the world, but words perform only up to a point. The mind performs only up to a point, since it's ultimately incapable of standing outside the sensations it receives and the judgments it forms from them. Aphorisms can sometimes suggest the nature of the riddle, but they won't solve it—another reason that readers who enjoy, and writers who indulge in, aphorisms gravitate toward irony. At bottom, existence is not explicable. One can take this state of affairs with glad grace, with uncomplaining fortitude, with various degrees of anger or melancholy, or with wry bemusement: "If you come to think of it," P. G. Wodehouse wrote, "what a queer thing Life is! So unlike anything else, don't you know?" Nor does the awareness of uncertainty guarantee the truth of statements about it. Wittgenstein's famous "Whereof one cannot speak, thereof one must be silent" seems to put the truth in a nutshell, but how do we know of what we cannot speak without first somehow articulating it to ourselves?

The authority we grant words makes communication possible. Nonetheless, there will always be a gap between language and truth. Propositions, Wittgenstein cautioned, reduce things to what we already know, and therefore using words to convey how words represent (i.e., distort) reality is like repairing "a torn spider's web with our fingers." If Wittgenstein, and Nietzsche before him, swerved from previous epistemological traditions, disavowing philosophical system-building, it was because they knew enough to do so. Their erudition crystallized into aphorisms. To a degree, all the important aphorists were both bookish and pedagogical. Poetry, it bears remembering, was a heuristic art meant to instruct as well as delight; and philosophy, or the love of wisdom, emerged to tell us how to apply such wisdom to life. The great aphorists—Bacon, La Rochefoucauld, Dr. Johnson, Hazlitt, Twain, Wilde, Shaw, and Orwell—didn't just spring up like roadside flowers; their roots reach back to Plato and Cicero.

History giveth and history taketh, and in this cycle it seems to have taken away the aphorism and given us the sound bite. One-liners from commercials, movies, TV shows, and popular songs abound—just check out the recently published and ridiculous *Yale Book of Quotations*, which includes such gems as "Free your mind and your ass will follow." A high quotability quotient, however, is no indication of aphoristic charm or depth. And although deep thinking is not required to compose aphorisms, a certain literary flair is, and lately the business of memorable phrase-making has fallen to copywriters and screenwriters. While it's nice to know that "We're all connected" and "A mind is a terrible thing to waste," it's sad to think that we no longer look to poets for the epigrams and aphorisms that define us. When did a poem last offer up a really memorable line about who we are or the age we live in?

I can speak only about American and British poetry, but I have to go back as far as Auden ("Those to whom evil is done/Do evil in return") and Larkin ("All solitude is selfish") to come up with lines worth reciting on these matters.

It's not as though we've given up on the aphorism. Geary's *World in a Phrase* sold well enough to warrant his demurely titled *Geary's Guide to the World's Great Aphorists,* which is a perfectly fine book to browse in, as long as you don't mind coming across such clunkers as "One dies of everything, mostly of living" and "Even damnation is poisoned with rainbows." Readers, evidently, still want healthy portions of wisdom delivered in small doses, but this alone does not guarantee the health of the aphorism. For that, we require writers who deliberately compose those self-contained, stick-in-your-mind pronouncements that were once a staple of the literary life. How many still do?

No one is to blame for this situation; culture is, after all, partially determined by what we expect from it. But since writers, especially novelists, cannot help but address the human condition, sooner or later one is bound to get lucky. As A.N. Whitehead observed, "It is a short step from a careless phrase to a flash of insight." Yes, it is. But, then, luck is often just the cap on experience and learning; that careless phrase could be gestating right now, and when the moment is right, the cap comes off and the words come out, one after another, in perfect marching order.

5

THE USUAL SUSPECT

Edgar Allan Poe, Consulting Detective

On the list of writers who have led thoroughly wretched lives Edgar Allan Poe must place near the top. Nor did he fare so well in death. A few days after his fatal collapse in 1849, an obituary, written by his literary executor Rufus A. Griswold, appeared in *The Daily Tribune:* "This announcement will startle many, but few will be grieved by it." Griswold then followed up with the *really* spiteful *A Memoir of the Author* which flat-out lied about Poe's character, drinking, and relations with women. Although a few writers came to Poe's defense, it would be another hundred years before people stopped seeing him as a drug-taking wastrel and degenerate. Eventually, thanks to the efforts of Joseph Wood Krutch, Julian Symons, the indefatigable Burton K. Pollin, and Dwight Thomas and David K. Jackson (whose amazing *The Poe Log* appeared in 1987), the tormented dreamer finally became the tormented but self-conscious professional writer, critic, and editor.

Biographies of more recent vintage have made good use of this material. Kenneth Silverman's 1992 book opened the curtains on a Freudian-driven Poe, who continually reenacts the loss of the mother; and Jeffrey Meyers's chronicle, published a year earlier, tracked a bloody-minded, career-driven Poe, who shoots himself in the foot every time he's about to win a race. If you want to know what a turbulent life consists of, learn about Poe's forty years on earth. His alcoholism, his antagonistic relationship with his step-father, his slowly dying wife, his perfervid imagination, his paranoia, his fixation on plagiarism, his messy relations with women, his megalomania, his acute sensitivity to slights, and his frustrated literary ambition all made him—shall we say?—a little testy.

Poverty alone almost did him in. "The Raven", which made him famous, netted him around nine dollars, and "The Gold Bug", which sold some quarter-million copies in his lifetime, earned him a whopping one hundred dollars. Poe worried incessantly about money, yet despite his troubles, both real and imagined, despite his binge-drinking and nettlesome and self-destructive behavior, his writings total nearly 2,900 pages in the two-volume *Library of America* series. It almost makes one believe that his genius was tied to his *tsuris*. He certainly thought himself a genius (only a man with impregnable self-esteem could appoint as his executor someone whose own writings he'd savaged in print). More to the point, it was Poe's obsession with genius that led to the creation of a new literary genre.

Although it's possible to argue about who wrote the first poem or the first novel, or who was the first to use stream-of-consciousness technique in fiction, there is no disputing who invented the formal detective story. Until "The Murders in the Rue Morgue" materialized in 1841, nothing like it had ever been seen. Literature had its share of plays and stories dealing with crime and punishment, but the intermediate step of figuring out "whodunit" had never come up. Audiences *knew* who'd poisoned the king or strangled the mistress because it either happened onstage or was described on the page. But with "The Murders in the Rue Morgue", readers encountered a tale that challenged them to guess the identity of the murderer.

Before Poe drew up the blueprint, criminous literature—say, William Godwin's *Caleb Williams* (1794) or Edward Bulwer-Lytton's *Eugene Aram* (1832)—was more concerned with society's flaws (which helped produce the criminal) than with the criminal's own flaws. Vice and virtue—not the modus operandi of the criminal or the police—were the cornerstones of their books. It wasn't until Eugène François Vidocq, a thief-turned-policeman, published his *Mémoires* in 1828 that attention began to be paid to the methods used to hunt down miscreants. Poe, however, didn't care a fig about the conditions that made the criminal or what motivated him, or even about how to apprehend him. What Poe cared about was the unriddling or the cerebral pursuit of truth. His innovation was to treat murder as a purely intellectual or aesthetic exercise; murder most foul could now become murder most ingenious.

Prior to Poe, not only was there no amateur detective; there were no literary heroes defined by their analytical intelligence. Odysseus was wily, Solomon wise, Falstaff shrewd, and Robinson Crusoe resourceful, but poets and writers didn't spend their time extolling or demonstrating the brainpower of their protagonists. In creating the chevalier C. Auguste Dupin, Poe gave us a hero who conspicuously *thinks* rather than feels, and who would be endlessly reconfigured by future generations of mystery writers.

Within the scope of five stories—"The Murders in the Rue Morgue", "The Mystery of Marie Rogêt", "The Purloined Letter", "The Gold-Bug", and "Thou Art the Man" (Dupin appears in the first three)—all the conventions of the formal detective story take shape. There is the genial and admiring narrator who somewhat uncomprehendingly follows the action; the consulting detective whose recondite interests and specialized knowledge make him superior to the local constabulary; the body discovered in a locked or "hermetically sealed" room; the trail of circumstantial evidence or false clues (red herrings) that point to the wrong man; the unlikely person who turns out to be the murderer; the seemingly trivial or irrelevant detail that holds the key to the mystery; and the unexpected stratagem the detective employs to solve the case. And, as all students of the mystery genre know, "The Murders in the Rue Morgue" introduced the two great principles of detective fiction: (1) When all impossible scenarios have been eliminated, then whatever remains, however improbable, must be the answer; and (2) The more bizarre the crime, the simpler its solution.

The formal detective story is basically one of delayed recognition. The reader ponders the same clues as the detective, but the moment of comprehension—the *Ah-ha!* instant of recognition—is kept in check by the detective's less intellectually nimble sidekick, the narrator. And therein lies the suspense. Now, suspense exists on some level in all novels—Will Elizabeth Bennet finally realize Darcy's true intentions? Will Jean Valjean continue to elude Javert?—but this depends more on the reader's investment in the characters than on the novelist's own designs. In the formal detective story, suspense is the point, with the author holding back the identity of the criminal and the reason for the crime in order to spring them on us at the end.

To purists of the mystery genre, a true mystery works best as short fiction, because once the detective is yoked to the novel, the art of observation and deduction begins to take a back seat to such novelistic concerns as the hero's background, the psychology of the criminal mind, and the familial or social forces that factor into the commission of a crime. As Poe saw it, and as Arthur Conan Doyle restated it, the pure story of detection is about problem-solving, not about solving the problems of society.

Poe's own considerable analytical abilities were first displayed in his article about a popular sideshow automaton capable of defeating human opponents. Poe's deduction in "Maelzel's Chess Player" wasn't earth-shattering (how many scenarios could there be?), but he brought to the table a methodology that was decidedly Dupin-like, including the intuitive leap that distinguishes a great from a merely competent logician. For Poe, genius wasn't characterized only by superior reasoning; it also required an imaginative component that enabled one person to see the figure in the carpet where others saw only colored fibers. When Poe described the analyst as "fond of enigmas, of conundrums, of hieroglyphics," he was speaking of himself. As the editor of various publications, he routinely challenged readers to send him cryptograms they thought beyond his abilities.

The casual reader of Poe's work may be aware that he created the amateur detective, yet how many know that he took it upon himself to solve a real crime by writing about it? The victim was a twenty-one-year-old New York woman by the name of Mary Cecilia Rogers, whose body was discovered on July 28, 1841 in the waters along the New Jersey shore, near Hoboken. The tragedy of her death and the sensation it created were enough to inscribe Mary's name in the annals of New York City history. But unless you're a student of that history, your knowledge of the murder has probably been filtered through "The Mystery of Marie Rogêt". In his recent survey of the case, *The Beautiful Cigar Girl*, Daniel Stashower writes that "[Poe's] story rose above the chaos that attended its composition and took on the air of established fact. Later critics would marvel over the manner in which Poe . . . solved a crime." In a sense, Poe did the murdered girl a disservice because as the years passed, the emphasis on the crime shifted from the facts to Poe's presentation of them; and Marie Rogêt gradually became more real than Mary Rogers. Although books about the murder have appeared sporadically—Raymond Paul's *Who Murdered Mary Rogers?* and Amy Gilman Srebnick's *The Mysterious Death of Mary Rogers*—it's hard, at least for mystery buffs, nor to see it through the eyes of Dupin.

Stashower's book is not quite sui generis, but it is different. *The Beautiful Cigar Girl* is an entertainingly offbeat and sometimes just-short-of-scholarly disquisition that nicely dovetails Poe's hectic life and stalled career into a civic lesson about old New York. It's part biography, part true crime, part history of tabloid journalism. Oddly, Stashower's detailed examination of the murder and Poe's involvement misses an essential point—namely, that without the confluence of those events—the factual and the fictional—the detective genre might have taken a different turn. Cold comfort, perhaps, to the shade of the murdered girl, but there it is: if Mary had lived out her life or if her murder had been resolved expeditiously, the character of Dupin, invented just three months earlier, might not have been reprised.

Mary Cecilia Rogers and Edgar Allan Poe both came to New York in 1837; she with her widowed mother from Lyme, Connecticut; he with his young wife and mother-in-law/aunt from Richmond, Virginia. Mary found a job as a shop girl in Anderson's Tobacco Emporium at 319 Broadway, while Poe, as usual, scrambled to make ends meet. Although respectable young women did not take jobs in male-dominated establishments, the Emporium's proprietor, John Anderson, promised Mary's mother that Mary would never be left alone and would always be escorted home. Whatever his other motives, Anderson figured that the dark-haired stunner would attract customers, whether they smoked or not. He was right. With Mary behind the counter, Anderson's store became a downtown back room for the journalists and politicos who worked nearby.

Because so many reporters hung out at the Emporium, "the comely seegar vendor" soon began to appear in their dispatches: "She's picked for her beauty from many a belle, / And placed near the window, Havanas to sell." Mary Rogers not only sold cigars but became something of a commodity herself, a precursor of today's celebrities whose only recommendation is being well known. "It is a most curious thing," one article noted, "Her notoriety is unencumbered by position or achievement." Mary wasn't the first American beauty, but she may have been the first to be celebrated so lavishly in print. And on October 6, 1838, her notoriety went up a notch when her mother found a suicide note on Mary's dressing-room table and hurriedly notified the police. Mary eventually showed up for work late that afternoon, but no one, it seemed, knew where she had been. Mary herself remained tight-lipped, which only fueled speculation. Had she been jilted? Was the suicide note a mean-spirited trick perpetrated by a lover whom *she'd* jilted? Or was it nothing more than a newspaper hoax? In time the commotion subsided. Mary continued to work at the cigar store, quitting only when her mother opened a boardinghouse on Nassau Street in the summer of 1839.

Poe never mentions running into Mary Rogers, but it's a good bet that he did. His stay in New York overlapped Mary's tenure at the cigar store, and though he lived in the West Village, he spent a fair amount of time downtown. Poe, a shameless literary operator, certainly stopped by the Shake-speare Tavern at the corner of Nassau and Fulton streets to talk shop with Washington Irving and James Fenimore Cooper, and he probably accompanied them uptown to the Tobacco Emporium, where they would have chatted up Horace Greeley and cast amorous glances at Mary Rogers.

In 1839, Poe left New York to take a job in Philadelphia and, in all likelihood, forgot about the beautiful cigar girl until his memory was jogged by her second disappearance. As before, the incident was shrouded in mystery. On the morning of July 25, which happened to be a Sunday, Mary purportedly told one of the tenants of the boardinghouse, a Mr. Daniel Payne, who later claimed to be her fiancé, that she was off to visit an aunt who lived some fifteen minutes away. A violent thunderstorm flared up that afternoon, and when Mary didn't return home, her mother and Payne assumed that she had stayed the night. But by late Monday afternoon, with no word from her, Payne placed a missing person's ad in the *New York Sun*.

Three days later a woman's waterlogged and battered body was towed to shore. The features were disfigured beyond recognition and the corpse, according to the coroner on the scene, was "nightmarish in its injuries." The body lay on the ground until Alfred Crommelin, a former boarder and would-be suitor of Mary's, rushed up and identified it by Mary's "delicate feet" and the "pattern of hair" growing on one of her arms. Later that day, the coroner would note "a mark about the size and shape of a man's thumb on the right side of the neck, near the jugular vein, and two or three marks on the left side resembling the shape of a man's fingers." The dress was torn in several places and a piece of it "was tied round her mouth, with a hard knot at the back part of the neck." Mary's bonnet, it seemed, had been removed and then replaced after death. Examining "the feminine region," the coroner found that Mary had been "brutally violated by no fewer then three assailants, and finally murdered"; and since "there was not the slightest trace of pregnancy," the victim "had evidently been a person of chastity and correct habits."

What had happened to Mary after she left the boardinghouse? Who had inflicted these terrible injuries, and why? Theories abounded, anonymous letters were sent to the authorities, and eyewitnesses stepped forward claiming to have seen Mary in various locations. Suspects, including Payne, Crommelin, a philandering husband, a young sailor, and even John Anderson were dragged in and questioned. All, however, were released for lack of evidence. Newspapers meanwhile whipped up readers' excitement with lurid details and spurious speculation. New York City in 1841 had numerous papers, including subscription offerings such as the *New York Evening Post*, standard weeklies such as the *New York Sunday Mercury*, and evening editions such as the *Tattler*. There were also the new "penny press" papers: Benjamin Day's *New York Sun*, James Gordon Bennett's *New York Herald*, and Horace Greeley's *New York Tribune* (which started up around the time of the murder). Depending on which paper one read, Mary had been killed by a secret lover, a rejected suitor, a madman, or by one of the vicious Five Point gangs that ruled downtown New York.

A month after the gruesome discovery, a new wrinkle appeared. A widow, Mrs. Frederica Loss, who owned a tavern in Weehawken, New Jersey, informed the Hoboken police that her sons had discovered articles of clothing in a nearby thicket. Recovered were a petticoat, a silk scarf, strips of fabric found hanging on a branch, a handkerchief with the initials M.R., and a parasol. For some reason, Mrs. Loss had withheld this information for an entire week before notifying anyone. Questioned by New Jersey magistrate Gilbert Merritt, she acknowledged that on June 25, a woman fitting Mary's description and a young man with a "swarthy" complexion had entered the tavern. They had a drink—he a glass of liquor, and she some lemonade—and a short time later walked down to the river. "The murder thicket," as the press termed it, now became the focus of the investigation. Signs of a violent struggle were found, but the newspapers still couldn't agree as to whether the murder was committed by one man or by a gang of "blacklegs and ruffians." Nor did the situation become clearer when, on October 7, Daniel Payne's hat was discovered lying in the murder thicket with Payne himself not far away, dying from an overdose of laudanum.

While all these events were transpiring in New York and Weehawken, Edgar Allan Poe was enjoying an interlude of relative prosperity. As editor of *Graham's Magazine* with an annual salary of $800, he was able temporarily to support his small family. Like everyone else who followed the Mary Rogers case, he didn't know what to make of it. At some point, however, when the investigation seemed to bog down, Poe decided to step in. In June of 1842 he sent a letter to a few magazines. His idea was ingenious, unheard of, even . . . postmodern. He would construct "a series of nearly exact *coincidences* occurring in Paris":

> Thus, under pretense of showing how Dupin . . . unravelled
> the mystery of Marie's assassination, I, in reality, enter into
> a very long and rigorous analysis of the New York tragedy.

No point is omitted. I examine, each by each, the opinions
and arguments of the press upon the subject, and show that
this subject has been, hitherto, *unapproached.*

Poe insisted that he would not only re-create the crime in
print but also tie up the loose ends and solve the real case by
having Dupin "sitting steadily in his accustomed armchair."
Dupin would gather the known facts as they had appeared in
newspapers and police and coroner's reports, and then, by
dint of ratiocination, demonstrate that Mary Rogers had been
killed by a lone assassin. Even though the case was still in the
public mind, the first two editors whom Poe approached
didn't bite. The format must have seemed a bit outré. Poe did
succeed, however, in attracting the interest of William Snowden, the editor of the incongruously sedate *Ladies' Companion.*
As it happened, Snowden had been among a group of promi-
nent New Yorkers who had convened after Mary's murder
to offer a reward for any information leading to her attacker.
He decided to publish "The Mystery of Marie Rogêt" in three
installments, the first two parts to run in the October and
November issues, and the denouement, identifying the killer,
to appear around the Christmas holidays.

A small confusion now occurs in Stashower's narrative. At
one point, Stashower writes that "the first two installments
had already appeared when new and disturbing evidence
surfaced in the case." Elsewhere, however, he notes that "Suddenly, on November 18, just as the second installment . . . was
due to appear, the name of Mary Rogers found its way back
onto the front pages." It's a minor discrepancy, though, and
shouldn't distract us from the fact that Poe had finished the
manuscript and that Dupin had "figured out" the identity of
Mary's killer *before* information came to light that derailed the

original investigation. The headline that must have given Poe a fit appeared in Horace Greeley's *New York Tribune*:

The Mary Rogers Mystery Explained

Once again it was the shady Mrs. Loss who stirred the pot. Having been accidentally shot by one of her sons in November, she confessed, on her deathbed, her true involvement in the case to Justice Merritt. According to the *Tribune*, Mary had come to Mrs. Loss's tavern with a young doctor to have an abortion performed. But the procedure went terribly wrong. Her body was then disposed of by Mrs. Loss and her three sons. This report, however, was immediately challenged by Merritt, who insisted that no such confession had been made owing to Mrs. Loss's "deranged state." On the other hand, Merritt himself filed an affidavit accusing Mrs. Loss and her sons of having been accessories to the murder. Although Merritt stopped short of stating what had happened, he referred to the tavern as "one of the most depraved and debauched houses in New Jersey."

If Mary had died during a botched abortion, the coroner who had examined her was clearly not well acquainted with the "feminine region," and Poe, who had relied on the coroner's report, was in trouble. It was too late to change what had already been published, but he could at least rework the third section, which was now rescheduled for February. Because no extant copies of Poe's pre-Weehawken-news manuscript exist, we can't be certain what his changes consisted of, but Stashower is an excellent guide and points to the spots where Poe most likely deviated from the original. While allowing for the possibility of an abortion, Poe sticks to his original conclusion that a naval officer, with whom Mary had been having an affair, was involved in her death. Poe certainly had every right to his opinion: not only was there no hard evidence of an abortion, the abortion scenario didn't explain all facets of the crime. Why, for example, were there ligature marks around the neck? Why the sailor's knot in the strings of the bonnet? And why were there signs of violence in the "murder thicket" if Mary had died indoors?

Poe would revisit the story, in 1845, upon its inclusion in a book published by Wiley & Putnam. He tinkered again with the ending and also revised the first two parts, adding a preliminary footnote stating that the author had knowledge of *"two* persons" who confirmed "absolutely all chief hypothetical details" which formed the author's conclusion. No corroboration for this rather audacious claim was ever produced, and so the matter rests. However Mary may have met her end, the scrutiny her death received spurred changes in public policy. In 1845, New York City instituted the Police Reform Act, which effectively modernized the city's police force; and that same year a law criminalizing abortion was passed by the state legislature.

Stashower's delving into the origins of Poe's story and his strict attention to Poe's hedgings will probably be of little interest to the general reader, though Stashower does his best at injecting drama into them. As for the drama of the plot itself, Dorothy Sayers suggests that connoisseurs of detective fiction will find "The Mystery of Marie Rogêt" the most rewarding of Poe's writings, which is another way of saying that one had better be a connoisseur before approaching it. The truth is that "Marie Rogêt" contains deep narrative ruts etched out by Dupin's meticulous rendering of the conflicting theories in the case. The story is told mostly through newspaper clippings from the "French press," and the action, such as it is, consists in Dupin's mulling over the facts and mewling over the newspapers' ineptness in interpreting them. The reader is treated to discourses on mildew, decay, drowning, the way fabric tears on branches, and the speed at which grass grows. Poe does make connections that the newspapers miss, but it's not enough to generate any real suspense. The game's afoot, but the detective's feet are tied to his chair.

The better story, in fact, may be the implicit one: what might have been if Mary Rogers hadn't died. A few months before Mary's second disappearance, Poe had published "The Murders in the Rue Morgue". It had been well received, but Poe had no plans for writing another detective story. For one thing, he didn't know that he *had* written one, since the word "detective" wasn't even in use in 1840.[1] Poe had simply, in his own words, devised a tale of ratiocination, "something in a new key." He had intended to carve out a place in literature for the analytical and imaginative thinker, and that's what he did.

There's nothing, then, to indicate that Poe was thinking of bringing Dupin back. Given his fascination with puzzles and problems of logic, he would have gone on to write "The Gold-Bug" and "Thou Art the Man", but it's not at all certain that he would have written another story featuring Dupin, in which case "The Purloined Letter" might never

---

[1] According to J. N. Gilbert's *Criminal Investigation*, Charles Dickens was the first to use "detective" in print in his "The Modern Science of Thief-Taking" (*Household Words*, July, 13, 1850). The OED, however, identifies the first usage as "detective policeman" in an 1843 article from *The Chamber's Journal*. The detective policeman is one "detailed quietly" to investigate a crime immediately after it occurs.

have been found. And without the three Dupin stories, who knows whether Arthur Conan Doyle would have conceived of Sherlock Holmes or seen him as a recurring figure? And *without* Holmes, the course of detective fiction is practically unimaginable.

In his essay "The Truth About Sherlock Holmes," Conan Doyle reveals that when he was casting about for something new to write, he thought of "Poe's masterful detective, M. Dupin . . . [and] of my old teacher Joe Bell, of his eagle face, of his curious ways . . . of his eerie trick of spotting details." Dr. Bell, as every Baker Street Irregular knows, was not only a Lecturer in Surgery at the Royal College of Surgeons of Edinburgh, but he was also Dr. Arthur Conan Doyle's mentor. It was Bell along with Dupin who nudged Doyle to create Sherlock Holmes, and it is Holmes who really begat the rest of them—the amateur detectives who found their way to our bedside tables: Jacques Futrelle's Professor Van Dusen a.k.a. "The Thinking Machine;"; G. K. Chesterton's Father Brown; Baroness Orczy's Old Man in the Corner; Agatha Christie's Hercule Poirot and Miss Marple; John Dickson Carr's Dr. Gideon Fell; Dorothy Sayer's Lord Peter Wimsey; Frederic Dannay and Manfred B. Lee's Ellery Queen; and Rex Stout's Nero Wolfe, to name just a few of the better-known sleuths. Charming, insufferable, autocratic, or eccentric—all derive from Poe's denizen of the Parisian night. And just as Dupin acknowledges his own literary precursor ("Vidocq . . . was a good guesser, and a persevering man . . . who impaired his vision by holding the object too close"), Holmes refers to Dupin as "a very inferior fellow . . . He had some analytical genius, no doubt; but he was by no means such a phenomenon as Poe appeared to imagine." The Holmesian ego cannot properly abide a competitor, but Doyle had no problem acknowledging his own debt to Poe: "If every man who receives a cheque for a story which owes its springs to Poe were to pay a tithe to a monument for the master, he would have a pyramid as big as that of Cheops."

Poe is one of those writers one is either passionately for or passionately against. The French symbolists thought Poe was just a letter away from being the perfect poet, but English-speaking critics have been put off by his parade of adjectives, rococo phrasings, and stark metaphorical road signs. Henry James, in fact, considered an enthusiasm for Poe "the mark of an extremely primitive stage of reflection," and Aldous Huxley remarked that coming across the poems was like encountering someone "wearing a diamond ring on every finger."

Although the Dupin stories also indulge Poe's taste for heightened language, they are usually overlooked in all the critical hullabaloo. There's a small irony here—because whatever one thinks of "The Black Cat" and "Annabel Lee", *they* did not have the literary implications of the five detective tales. (No major novelists or poets, after their juvenilia phase, took as a starting point the poems or horror stories.) But just as all modern Russian novels, in the words of Dostoevsky, emerged from under Gogol's "The Overcoat", so all mysteries— the innumerable British cozies and their European, Australian, African, and American spin-offs—emigrated from the Rue Morgue. If Conan Doyle was capable one hundred years ago of referring to "the monstrous progeny of writers on the detection of crime," there must be enough around today to populate a small country.

This is, of course, the very reason that the Popular Culturists find Poe so rewarding. They've managed to disinter or deconstruct the Freudian Poe, the Jungian Poe, the Lacanian, the phenomenological, and whatever other "deep" Poe lies beneath the semiotic layers of his prose. Detective stories certainly contain their share of implicit social and psychological insight, but aside from the underlying Victorian optimism that characterized the genre's beginnings—the triumph of reason, the punishment of evil, the advancement of civilization—it's hard to say what a Dupin story really means. Poe simply, startlingly, ushered in a new kind of hero and a new way of telling a story, beginning with a crime, then demonstrating the order and causality of the events that led up to it. The first detective stories may have held a mirror up to society, but their primary order of business was to place a somewhat obtuse narrator in the company of a superior intellect and follow that intellect's progress toward truth. And there is something both logically and emotionally satisfying in experiencing this, especially when the detective, like Oedipus, steps forward to "bring what is dark to light."

6

A MAN FOR ALL REASONS

Jacques Barzun

When Jacques Barzun, freshly armed with a Ph.D. in 1932, announced that he intended to write a history of Europe, the director of the Bibliothèque Nationale took him aside. "Wait until you're eighty," he advised the twenty-five-year-old scholar. Barzun thought it over, and thought it over, and then waited until he was nearly ninety to begin. In June of 2000 the fruit of that thinking, *From Dawn to Decadence: 500 Years of Western Cultural Life*, appeared on *The New York Times* Best-Sellers List. (Barzun's other book to reach the list, *The House of Intellect*, ascended in 1959, making the interval between appearances—forty-one years—a record.) Encountering *From Dawn to Decadence* between titles by Dr. Laura Schlessinger (late of the airwaves) and Shirley MacLaine (of ancient Sumeria and environs) was a bit like having a whale nose up to you in an aquarium. Who expected an eight-hundred-page cultural history, ranging from Ficino to Johnny Rotten, to be so commercial?

This, of course, says more about the cyclical nature of intellectual fashion than about Barzun's industriousness. Barzun, who is now approaching his 104th birthday, is the author of thirty-seven books and the editor or translator of fourteen others. His name is most closely associated with Columbia University, where he taught history for forty-eight years, and with Lionel Trilling, with whom he conducted a famous colloquium on the Great Books. Although he retired in 1975, he has not ceased doing battle with those determined to hang the vast historical brocade on an ideological frame.

Barzun eschews ideology—of any stripe. Grand theories or immaculate systems seeking to apprehend experience are anathema to him, and he regards their progenitors as "imperialists who want the entire cosmos drawn like a wire through their single keyhole." Nor does he spend much time pondering timeless questions about life and death. Like William James, his favorite philosopher, Barzun grapples with metaphysical questions in order to demonstrate that thought is best served by grappling with experience. The two men are a temperamental fit. When James wrote, "I am no lover of disorder, but fear to lose truth by the pretension to possess it entirely," he might as well have been speaking for Barzun. "Damn the Absolute," James thundered, and damn it Barzun has.

There *is*, however, a philosophical—even an existential—component to Barzun's writings. "The purpose I gradually fashioned," he acknowledged thirty years ago, "took the form of a resolve to *fight the mechanical*," by which he mean any ossified system of beliefs and the behaviors based on them. Our great mistake, according to Barzun, is that we try to affect mechanically what is actually a condition—the human one:

"The supposition is that what we face is a problem to be solved; and it is a foolish supposition," Barzun wrote. "Human affairs rarely contain problems with solutions. They contain predicaments and difficulty, which is a very different thing." And because life "overflows ideologies and coercive systems" and makes everything possible (including ideologies and coercive systems), he views our span on earth not as something to engineer to our advantage, but as a natural state whose unpredictability we must adapt to.

Pointedly, Barzun refers at least twice in his writings to Faulkner's 1950 Nobel Prize address, which contends that, "If a writer has to rob his mother, he will not hesitate: the 'Ode to a Grecian Urn' is worth any number of old ladies." Not so, Barzun counters. "It is old women, not Grecian urns, that have in their time borne Keatses and Faulkners." Barzun not only objects to an art-for-art's-sake philosophy; he also wants us to know what it *really* means: it is at bottom an art-for-life's-sake philosophy, which makes it just another attempt to reduce the richness and complexity of existence.

This is not what a literary intellectual is supposed to feel, but then Barzun doesn't care for the word "intellectual," believing it gets misused too often. Nor does he like "academic." "Educator," too, is off limits, since a person's education is acquired in spite of formal schooling. Barzun, prefers the humbler "teacher" or the not-so-humble "pedagogue," which literally means leading someone to knowledge. Jacques Barzun may be the author of *Teacher in America* and *The American University*, yet he shares Oscar Wilde's anxiety about finding himself "seated next to a man who has spent his life in trying to educate others."

Barzun is a cultural historian, plain and simple, except that nothing about culture or history is plain or simple.

> History, like a vast river, propels logs, vegetation, rafts, and
> debris; it is full of live and dead things, some destined for
> resurrection; it mingles many waters and holds in solution
> invisible substances stolen from distant soils. Anything
> may become part of it; that is why it can be an image of the
> continuity of mankind. And it is also why some of its freight
> turns up again in the social sciences: they were constructed
> out of the contents of history in the same way as houses in
> medieval Rome were made out of stones taken from the
> Coliseum. But the special sciences based on sorted facts
> cannot be mistaken for rivers flowing in time and full of
> persons and events. They are systems fashioned with con-
> cepts, numbers, and abstract relations. For history, the
> reward of eluding method is to escape abstraction.

As an historian Barzun has trained himself to take the long
view. For him, the present, no matter how fraught, is always
seen in light of old turmoils. Whatever events and ideas are
currently polarizing the chattering classes are simply part of
the parade; they, too, shall pass. Consequently, there's nothing
Hegelian, Heideggerian, or hermeneutic about his work; no
nihilistic or existential angst livens things up. Histories that
impart a unifying design in the categorical manner of Spengler's organic cycle of regional growth and decay, or Braudel's
emphasis on broad socioeconomic "structures" are not his kind
of history. Indeed, he considers any systematic model of cause
and effect to run counter to the historical temper, which, in his
view, is intuitive, concrete, and beholden to time and evidence.
History on the page is not a proof but an interpretive art that
negotiates among, and accesses, great mounds of information;
and any attempt to graft a system on to what is really a series of
multifarious events is doomed to fail.

How, then, is one to interpret what happens? If you're Jacques Barzun you read everything that has been written and commit it to memory. Barzun's breadth of erudition has been a byword among friends and colleagues for over seven decades. He always seemed to know everything you had read or thought about reading, and he was just as comfortable talking about German architecture as about Venetian politics. Like Mycroft Holmes (Sherlock's older brother), he was someone to whom experts turned for help in *their* fields. Among his areas of expertise are French and German literature, music, education, ghost stories, detective fiction, language, and etymology. He has, of course, read every historian worth mentioning, while also managing to examine Poe as proofreader, Abraham Lincoln as stylist, Diderot as satirist, and Liszt as reader. In addition to assessing the writings of Rousseau, Darwin, Marx, Ruskin, and Shaw, he has burnished the reputations of such lesser known writers as Thomas Beddoes, James Agate, and John Jay Chapman. "He was terrifying," Steven Marcus, a former dean of Columbia College, recalled about his undergraduate days. "He would disgorge an absolutely enormous amount of information during his lectures, more than anyone could possibly remember, and what you felt was—you felt you couldn't compete. I mean, you could imagine maybe one day writing something on the order of Trilling—maybe. But how could you ever know as much as Barzun did?"

The charge against Barzun, accordingly, is that he has spread himself too thin. Surely a familiarity with so many subjects precludes a depth of knowledge about any one of them. It was this polymathic quality that caused him to be taken less seriously by the academic pashas who ran the major literature departments and literary quarterlies in the

1970s and 1980s. Barzun, though, never intended to write for that crowd. Instead, he wanted "to write for a quite different, less homogeneous group: academics in other departments than English, people with a non-professional interest in the arts (doctors who play music, lawyers who read philosophy) and a certain number of men and women in business and philanthropy, in foundations and newspapers or publishing houses."

Barzun wanted to do on the page what he did in the classroom: help the reader "carry in his head something more than the unexamined history of his own life," not because knowledge is inherently good or makes one a better person but because it fosters an independence of mind. The more one learns about the course of civilization, he maintained, the more one can appreciate its achievements. After a while, if you learn enough, you can argue that, say, Shaw's mind more closely resembles Rousseau's than Voltaire's—and you may actually enjoy doing it.

When I first met Barzun in January of 1970, he was sixty-two and I was twenty-two. He was the University Professor of History at Columbia; I was a first-year graduate student in the English and Comparative Literature Department. He lived on upper Fifth Avenue; I lived in the Bronx, near Kingsbridge Avenue. He attended the opera; I hung out at revival movie theaters. He wore bespoke suits; I didn't own a suit. He said "potato"; I said "pot." There was no reason we should have gotten along. To him I was just a student in a green Army jacket who smoked filterless Camels. To me he was just someone who had written the introduction to my Bantam edition of *Germinal*. And the fact that we did get along speaks more to his equanimity than to my dazzling personality. Indeed, I was the intolerant one. During the first years of our acquaintance, I thought he occasionally spent his time and intellect on matters beneath him. Why should a man who could write so capably about William James, who knew Montaigne backwards and forwards, bother himself with methods of research or the problems of receiving a decent secondary education? The man had the *Complete Works of John Ruskin* on his shelves, for heaven's sake; he could make the case that Flaubert's grammar and syntax were slovenly; he had read *Faust Part II* (*no one* reads Part II except German majors). Weren't there better things for him to write than *Simple and Direct*, a primer for writers?

Barzun, however, goes where he pleases, and despite the degrees and awards (he was made a Chevalier de l'Ordre National de la Légion d'Honneur and has received the Presidential Medal of Freedom), he has always regarded himself as an "amateur" (the Latin root, *amator* means "lover"), someone who takes genuine pleasure in what he learns about. Perhaps more than any other historian of the past four generations, Barzun has stood for the seemingly contradictory ideas of scholarly rigor and unaffected enthusiasm. One of those enthusiasms produced what may be his most frequently quoted sentence: "Whoever wants to know the heart and mind of America had better learn baseball." The line, extracted from his book *God's Country and Mine*, is inscribed on a plaque at the Baseball Hall of Fame and routinely trotted out by news anchors and NPR commentators. Because of it he was once identified on the CBS Evening News as "a French philosopher." Barzun will, on occasion, mutter (in his articulate way) that after his books go out of print, no one will remember anything but those fourteen words about baseball.

Not everything that Barzun wrote struck me with equal force; at times I thought his style was too flat, too spare, especially when addressing complex subjects. Consequently, when he asked me to edit a compilation of his essays, I made so bold as to tinker with his prose. The editorial process led to a spate of letters, highlighting our asynchronous temperaments. During one exchange, I suggested that the importance of what he was saying warranted heightened language. His reply came so fast that I thought he'd bounded across Central Park and put the letter in my mailbox himself. "You are a sky-high highbrow," he wrote. "Me, I suspect highbrows (and low- and middle-) as I do all specialists, suspect them of making things too easy for themselves; and like women with a good figure who can afford to go braless, I go about brow-less." Undeterred, I offered to rewrite the passages in question. My changes were acknowledged with fitting tribute. "To put it in a nice, friendly, unprejudiced way," he responded, "your aim as shown in your rewritings of the 'objectionable' sentences strikes me as patronizing, smarmy, emetic!" Nonetheless, he rewrote the sentences to his own satisfaction, which, of course, is all an editor can expect.

With regard to his style, one might note that the historian and the critic have distinctive voices. When Barzun is compressing great batches of information, his prose races across spatial and chronological vistas, delivering facts, their causes and implications, in a strictly utilitarian, almost rat-a-tat manner. When he's addressing an artist's work, however, the prose becomes redolent, more capacious, its syntactical flourishes a tacit reflection of real appreciation. Very few historians could so confidently gauge a writer's mind:

> Shaw knows at any moment, on any subject, what he
> thinks, what you will think, what others have thought,

what all this thinking entails . . . Shaw is perhaps the most
consciously conscious mind that has ever thought—certainly the most conscious since Rousseau; which may be
why both of them often create the same impression of insincerity amounting to charlatanism.

One of the reasons that Barzun is fond of him is that he
approves of Shaw's disapproval of "modern" society. Barzun's own declinist views about Western civilization were
formed at the beginning of the modernist movement—as a
child he played in Duchamp's studio and attended the orches-
tral opening of Stravinsky's "Le Sacre du Printemps"— and
he has yet to come around to the cultural aftermath. Indeed,
for half a century he has maintained that "the forms of art as
of life seem exhausted" and that "the high creative energies"
of the Renaissance dissipated during the first quarter of the
twentieth century. Indeed, he's inclined to regard the provo-
cations of later modernist and postmodernist artists from
John Cage to Damien Hirst as leaves from a tree that was
planted before the First World War.

Jacques Barzun was born outside Paris in 1907. He was six
when the First World War broke out, and early on he sensed
that "a civilization," in Paul Valéry's harsh aperçu, "has the
same fragility as a life." The war shattered the world that he
knew and, as he later wrote, "visibly destroyed that nursery
of living culture." This isn't entirely a figure of speech.
On Saturdays before the war, his parents' living room had
been a raucous salon where many of Europe's leading avant-
garde artists and writers gathered: Varèse played the piano,
Ozenfant and Delaunay debated, Cocteau told lies, and Apol-
linaire declaimed. Brancusi often stopped by, as did Léger,

Kandinsky, Jules Romains, Duchamp, and Pound. But after 1914, when the shells began to fall, the visits gradually ceased; and soon came the names of the dead. His parents tried to conceal the losses, but the boy became depressed and, as he learned later, began hinting at suicide. At the age of ten, his parents bundled him off to the seashore at Dinard, where he immersed himself in Shakespeare and James Fenimore Cooper.

It's tempting to relate Barzun's skepticism about recent cultural developments to the intensity of his childhood milieu and its abrupt disappearance. Barzun readily acknowledges that the accident of birth is "bound to have irreversible consequences," but he rejects the idea that his character or sense of the world derives from any loss that he might have suffered as a child. In fact, when I broached the possibility that his precise way of formulating ideas and strict attention to empirical evidence are distinctive qualities of the civilization that he saw disintegrate before his eyes, his response was gently quizzical. "Why must you find trauma where there is none?" he asked. "I grew up a child of a bourgeois family, with emancipated parents who surrounded themselves with people who talked about ideas. My views were formed by my parents, by the lycée, and by my reading. How else should I be?"

With the war over, Barzun's father, the poet and diplomat Henri Martin Barzun, offered his only son a choice of completing his studies in England or in America. Barzun, with visions of Chingachgook dancing in his head, didn't hesitate, and in 1920 the family settled for a while in New Rochelle. Barzun, with the aid of tutors, entered Columbia at fifteen. His student life presaged his professional one. He majored in history, reviewed theatre for the daily *Spectator*, edited the monthly literary magazine, became the president of the Philolexian Society, and, together with his friend Wendell Hertig Taylor, kept a running tally of every mystery book that came along. Their brief descriptions, scribbled on three-by-five-inch index cards, eventually coalesced into *A Catalogue of Crime*, one of the foremost reference works in the mystery-suspense genre. He also managed to graduate as valedictorian of his class, a feat he considers less impressive than having written the 1928 Varsity Show, "Zuleika, or the Sultan Insulted."

Barzun joined the history faculty a year after graduating, at a moment when British and American universities, despite a general dislike of things Teutonic, were in thrall to the ideal of *Wissenschaft*, or scientific knowledge. Philosophers such as Wilhelm Dilthey had argued that history was a succession of conceptual forms and styles, capable of being classified and studied methodically. (Another German, of course, had maintained that class struggle was actually the transformative force behind historical events.) History was now thought too serious to be left to biographers and storytellers; and even Lord Acton urged his students to "study problems in preference to periods." Barzun, though hardly a practitioner of the old popes-and-princes school of history (his first books examined ideas about race and freedom), disapproved of attempts to refashion history as a social science. History wasn't "a piece of crockery dredged up from the Titanic," he wrote; it was, "first, the shipwreck, then a piece of writing."

He demanded, therefore, that historical narrative include "the range and wildness of individuality, the pivotal force of trifles, the manifestations of greatness, the failures of unquestioned talent." His models were Burkhardt, Gibbon, Macaulay, and Michelet, authors of imperfect mosaics characterized by a strong narrative line. As for philosopher-historians like Vico, Herder, and Spengler, Barzun held that they did not, despite creating prodigious works of learning, write histories at all: "It is not a paradox to say that in seeking a law of history those passionate minds were giving up their interest in history."

At Columbia, Barzun found a genial host for his far-flung interests. In addition to the broadly conceived Contemporary Civilization course, Columbia offered a General Honors class—later, the Colloquium on Important Books—that let a select group of upperclassmen read the Western classics with instructors from two fields. When Barzun was assigned to the Colloquium, in 1934, his teaching partner was the English instructor Lionel Trilling. Among the most influential literary critics to emerge from the academy, Trilling admitted late in life that he had once stood "puzzled, abashed, and a little queasy" before the "high artistic culture of the modern age," a discomfort no doubt torqued by sitting at a table next to a man whose mind had been formed at first hand by that culture. The Colloquium, as the word implies, was a conversation, and in 1934 it became not merely a conversation between instructors and undergraduates but also a dialogue between the two men that lasted until Trilling's death, in 1975.

Dissimilar in many respects, the urbane, Americanized Frenchman, with his easy manner, and the shy, intense, Jewish writer-aspirant from Queens, who had only recently renounced his Marxist views, soon shared their thoughts, showed each other drafts of their work, and gradually began to carve out a new discipline in American education. They broadened the critical spectrum to include the biographical and social conditions attending the creation of any cultural artifact, and rerouted the notion of individuality or genius toward a busy intersection where various historical forces converged.

Barzun and Trilling, it could be said, also broadened each other. One day in the mid-1930s, they began talking about novelists, and Barzun mentioned his admiration for Henry James. Trilling, who had read only a few of James's stories, replied that he thought him not much more than a "social twitterer." Barzun pressed upon him *The Pupil* and, as he recalls, *The Spoils of Poynton*. Trilling was duly persuaded, and marched off to convince Phillip Rahv and William Phillips, the editors of *Partisan Review*, that James was a writer to be taken seriously—and within five or six years he was.

In the Colloquium, books and ideas were thrown open to discussion, and almost every approach was tolerated. "Cultural criticism" was Barzun and Trilling's coinage for their lack of method, and it worked so well that in the mid-1950s Fred Friendly, an executive producer at CBS News, tried (and failed) to persuade the two men to offer a version of the Colloquium for television. The class met on Wednesday evenings and, as the decades passed and more specialized approaches to literature emerged, Barzun and Trilling remained committed to the essential messiness of culture. Neither the self-isolating pieties of the New Critics, nor the technical proficiency of the Russian Formalists, nor the class-bound shibboleths of Marxist writers held sway in their classroom. As a result, they were condemned, as Barzun recalled, "for overlooking the autonomy of the work of art and its inherent indifference to meaning; for ignoring the dialectic of history," not to mention "the 'rigorous' critical methods recently opened to those who could count metaphors, analyze themes, and trace myths."

Basically, Barzun and Trilling cast themselves in the Arnoldian mold of relating culture to conduct. Matthew Arnold believed that judging books "as to the influence which they are calculated to have upon the general culture" would help realize man's better nature and, thus, eventually improve society itself. Trilling and Barzun were less sanguine about the critic's power, but, like Arnold, they saw no fissure between moral and aesthetic intelligence. They interpreted books liberally and wrote about them with a fluency and a precision befitting R. P. Blackmur's definition of criticism as "the formal discourse of an amateur."

For all that, Barzun was never a "New York intellectual." He occasionally fraternized with the *Partisan Review* crowd, but he avoided the sectarian wars that seemed to fuel their lives and work; he appears only marginally in most accounts of the literary figures who rotated around the magazine. Yet when *Time* magazine ran a lead article about "America and the Intellectual" in the summer of 1956, it wasn't Edmund Wilson, or Lionel Trilling, or Sidney Hook, or Mark Van Doren whose likeness appeared on the cover (though all were mentioned inside); it was that of a man who hadn't even been born here.

Around 1941, Barzun took on a larger classroom, becoming the moderator of the CBS radio program "Invitation to Learning," which aired on Sunday mornings and featured four or five intellectual lights discussing books. From commenting on books, it was, apparently, a short step to selling them. In 1951, Barzun, Trilling, and W. H. Auden started up the Readers' Subscription Book Club, writing monthly appreciations of books that they thought the public would benefit from reading. The club lasted for eleven years, partly on the strength of the recommended books, which ranged from Kenneth Grahame's *The Wind in the Willows* to Hannah Arendt's *The Human Condition*, and partly on the strength of the editors' reputations.

Barzun's public reputation was made in 1943 with the appearance of *Romanticism and the Modern Ego*. The book defied prevailing opinion by arguing that the difference between the ostensibly unruly Romantic movement and the ostensibly neoclassical Enlightenment was fundamentally social and political, not aesthetic. "The Romanticists' point was in fact not an emotional point at all," Barzun claimed, "but an intellectual point about the emotional life of man." It was a bold statement to make at a time when Eliot's condescensions to the early-nineteenth-century poets dominated literature departments, and perhaps it took a historian to recognize that Eliot's distrust of personality and radicalism caused him to misjudge the Romantics' debt to, among others, Rousseau and Kant. As Barzun laid it out, Romanticism was no aberrant aesthetic movement but reflected an intellectual sensibility perfectly suited to a hectic and idealistic age. In short, he helped make Romanticism respectable.

Although Barzun's influence on literary studies is difficult to assess, there's little doubt about his role in the revival of Hector Berlioz. Barzun had heard Berlioz's "Ballet of the Sylphs" at a children's concert in Paris when he was four or five, and, nearly forty years later, when putting the finishing touches on his biography of the composer, he noticed that the French and German scores of "Roméo et Juliette" contained a small discrepancy. (The placing of mutes on the strings at one point in the Love Scene was different.) He happened to mention this to Toscanini's assistant, and a few days later he was having tea at Toscanini's house in Riverdale, discussing music in general and Berlioz's instrumentation and harmonics in particular.

Toscanini was one of a small number of musicians at midcentury who admired Berlioz. The rest of the music world, along with "conservatives, clerics, liberals and socialists," Barzun wrote, "all joined in repudiating" the Romantic style. But, where others heard in Berlioz disorder and bombast, Barzun discerned exuberance, vividness, and dramatic flair. When *he* listened to Berlioz, Barzun heard "Gothic cathedrals, the festivals of the Revolution, the antique grandeur of classic tragedy, the comic force of Molière and Beaumarchais, and the special lyricism of his own Romantic period." Barzun didn't just like Berlioz's music; he liked the mind that made the music, and his two-volume *Berlioz and the Romantic Century* (1950) not only spurred revisionist studies of Berlioz but also brought his music back into a general repertoire. "When I left school, I had to educate myself, and Jacques Barzun was part of my education," the British conductor Sir Colin Davis told me. Davis had lobbied for Berlioz's music in England, and in 1969 he conducted a magnificent performance of "Les Troyens" in London that eventually led to his recording all Berlioz's major works.

As much as he wrote about music and literature, Barzun was no unworldly aesthete, and his practical and political side was put to the test in 1958, when he assumed the inaugural post of provost and dean of faculties at Columbia. He remained provost for ten years and is generally credited with extricating the university from its financial and administrative woes. He also replaced the music played at graduation with the march from "Les Troyens."

Barzun returned to teaching the history of Western civilization just as it was coming under attack by various Continental theorists, whose repudiation of hierarchical structures and determinate meaning challenged everything that Barzun believed in. In the 1970s and 1980s, Barzun became a symbol of the Old Guard, a mandarin scholar futilely defending the works of dead white males. Even as late as 1990, he had a walk-on in Henry Louis Gates, Jr.'s spoof of the Culture Wars, which appeared in the *New York Times Book Review*. Barzun, dressed in evening clothes and packing a .38 Beretta, is, unsurprisingly, holding forth on standards and errors of usage.

In truth, Barzun looked the part of someone who embodied tradition. He stood a straight-up six feet two inches and wore clothes that, if not expensive, looked expensive on him. His hair was silver, his forehead high and broad, and his nose long and straight, with a slight dip at the end. He looked ambassadorial and possessed an air of authority that had less to do with giving orders than with the expectation that he would be listened to. Carolyn Heilbrun, one of the first female professors in Columbia's English and Comparative Literature Department, remembers that she felt patronized by Trilling and other male faculty, but she writes about Barzun almost reverently:

> No picture of him I have seen, whether rendered by a photographer or by an artist, captures either his physical or his inner qualities. Obvious to the mere observer or the frightened student were his aristocratic way of carrying himself, suggesting arrogance, his impeccable clothes, his neat hair, his studious, exact, but never hesitant speech, his formidable intelligence. I have known history students tempted for the first time in their lives to plagiarize a paper because they could not imagine themselves writing anything that would not affront his critical eye, let alone satisfy him.

And yet Barzun is not all genteel restraint, something that Sir Colin Davis touched on when speaking about Barzun's appreciation of Berlioz: "Such an interesting figure, Berlioz—so intelligent and self-conscious, but also volatile and passionate. I rather think Jacques is like that—his *internal* life, I mean, not his personal life." Barzun's prose may not give off much heat, but over and over one finds paeans to pure feeling, to the sensuous response to experience. Like William James, Barzun believes that feeling is at the root of all philosophy and art. "The greatest artists have never been men of taste," Barzun wrote, with Berlioz in mind. "By never sophisticating their instincts they have never lost the awareness of the great simplicities, which they relish both from appetite and from the challenge these offer to skill in competition with popular art." Because Barzun is so coolly analytical in his own work, one might infer that he would be drawn to poets of fine discrimination, to ingenious symbolists like Mallarmé and Valéry, and yet it's the rude vitality of Molière and Hugo that engages him.

Obvious emotionalism is not the point; it's the courage to be emotional that matters. Barzun has observed that "the vulgarity of mankind," in the sense of the common man's intense awareness of life—life with all its brief pleasures and bruising shocks—"is not only a source of art but the ultimate one." It's easy enough to understand why people don't immediately see this side of Barzun, and pass over, without notice, sentiments such as "And when will art cease to be something so exclusively for nice people?" or "Reading history remakes the mind by feeding primitive pleasure in story."

That's the problem with Barzun: he wriggles—a dignified wriggle, to be sure—out from under labels. A staunch defender of the canon, he advised against "a curriculum entirely made up of great books." A scholar who helped establish the humanities curriculum at Columbia, he discerns a clear distinction between the humanities and scholarship about them. A man of palpable reserve, he has written dozens of clerihews as well as a wink-wink monologue in the voice of Molly Bloom. (In Barzun's riff, she's married to Allan *The-Closing-of-the-American-Mind* Bloom and she's bothered by some of her "second" husband's ideas. And though a self-professed cultural historian, Barzun is convinced that culture proper belongs outside the university.

Contradictions, however, do not so much define him as simply call attention to his unfettered attitude toward experience. Among the things that drew him to William James was James's notion of the mind as a "thinking stream" that collected impressions without grading them (though that would follow). On a certain level, therefore, all experience is equal and deserves consideration. James himself, one will recall, was open to the possibilities of spiritualism, psychic evidence, and the theories of Freud. Barzun, too, tends not to dismiss much unless it smacks of stupidity or profundity, both of which he thinks we can do with less of.

He also subscribes to James's assessment that every reasonable request incurs a moral obligation in the claimant. This weirdly egotistical notion that the granting of the smallest request helps "moralize" the universe struck a chord with Barzun—and, as many budding writers or tenured professors can attest, Barzun was usually a soft touch; he'd read your manuscripts, even if they were five-hundred pages long.

I don't bring this up to praise him, but to convey what I think of as his conscience with regard to both social and intellectual obligations. As mentioned, he possesses a confounding equanimity. What self-respecting scholar doesn't want to get into a scholarly fracas? What kind of critic says that "Resentment is a form of ego I detest"? That's not an intellectual speaking, it's the Dalai Lama. And yet it is all part and parcel of a neurological and temperamental constitution that enabled him to amass great sums of learning and to portion it out in his varied works.

The man simply knows more than you do. This is a statement I am prepared to back up. Students and colleagues are not the only ones who have been startled by what he knows. The writer Shirley Hazzard, whose husband Francis Steegmuller had been a classmate of Barzun's, recalled an evening in the mid-1970s, when she and Barzun found themselves standing in a storage room on East Seventy-Ninth Street, up to their necks in books. They had been asked by the head librarian of the New York Society Library to help him weed out superfluous and out-of-date volumes. "There we were," Hazzard said, holding a hand at eye level, "standing among books stacked this high, and I thought, We're really in for it. We'll never get through these. Then Jacques reached into a pile, glanced at the title—it didn't matter which book it was— and said, 'This one's been superseded by another; this one is still valid; this one can stay until someone or somebody finishes his new study,' and in a couple of hours we were done. It was a very impressive performance, because, you know, he wasn't performing at all. It's just Jacques."

Sooner or later, all of Barzun's acquaintances experience their own "just Jacques" moment. Some years ago, while working on a piece about *the night*, I called Barzun to check whether Lord Edward Grey, the British Foreign Secretary during the First World War, had said that the lamps were going out all over Europe before hostilities had actually begun. Barzun asked if I was referring to him in my article as "Lord Grey." I said I was, since the attribution was always the same. Barzun cleared his throat. "Well, you know, he wasn't a lord when he said it. He didn't become Viscount of Fallodon until 1916." For the first time in thirty-odd years of conversation, I exclaimed, "Why would you know that?" He replied, mildly, "It's my business to know such things."

7

EN GARDE!

The Duel in History

On the night of June 10, 1804, Alexander Hamilton seated himself at his desk in his home in upper Manhattan to finish a letter explaining why the following morning would find him in Weehawken, New Jersey, pointing a flintlock pistil at Vice President Aaron Burr. He began by listing five moral, religious, and practical objections to duelling, but ruefully concluded, seven paragraphs later, that "what men of the world denominate honor" made it impossible for him to "decline the call." Burr had placed him in an untenable position. If Hamilton ignored the challenge, Burr would "post" him—that is, publish his refusal in the newspapers—and his political career would effectively be ruined. The next morning, Hamilton had himself rowed across the Hudson.

"If we were truly brave, we should not accept a challenge; but we are all cowards," a friend of Hamilton's said after his death. He was thinking not only of Hamilton but of all men in public life whose reputations were at the mercy of political rivals and incendiary journalism.[1] Hamilton, too, had issued challenges and seconded other men and, in one way or another, had been involved in more than ten "affairs of honor." Meanwhile, Burr had been party only to three duels, including one where he actually took the field. Neither man was an exception among the Founding Fathers. Button Gwinnet, a signer of the Declaration of Independence, died of wounds received in a duel; and James Monroe refrained from challenging John Adams only because Adams was president at the time. Some years later, Andrew Jackson and Henry Clay took part in duels, and even the young Abraham Lincoln came very close to a sword fight with James Shields, a fellow-Illinoisan who eventually became a Union general.

Duelling is an anachronism, of course. This is true because it may still crop up. In 1954, Ernest Hemingway was challenged to a duel in Cuba (he declined). In 1967, two French politicians literally crossed swords in Neuilly. And four years ago a Peruvian legislator challenged his nation's vice president to meet him on a beach near Lima. No one anticipates such shenanigans at Buckingham Palace, but the Queen, as it happens, still retains an official champion who stands ready to challenge anyone who disputes her sovereignty.

This rather daunting fact turns up in James Landale's *The Last Duel: A True Story of Death and Honor*. Landale, a correspondent for the BBC, is descended from one of the two men who fought the last recorded fatal duel on Scottish soil. Relying on a trial transcript, newspaper accounts, bank documents, and the correspondence of the duellists, Landale elegantly

---

[1] In his indispensable *The Duel in European History*, V. G. Kiernan makes the point that newspapers were part of the dueling culture. Duels helped sell papers, and inflammatory copy often generated challenges, often to the publisher himself. Reviewing an 1836 French book on dueling, a British writer might have experienced a twinge of discomfort in noting that "the journalist must make up his mind to a duel as one of the incidents of his profession."

reconstructs the circumstances that forced his ancestor David Landale, at the mature age of thirty-nine, to challenge his former banker, George Morgan. David Landale, a linen merchant from the coastal town of Kirkcaldy, just north of Edinburgh, was, if anything, more reluctant than Hamilton to pick up a pistol; he didn't even own one. But the code of honor extended to wherever men conducted business, and honor dictated that Landale challenge Morgan. The two met in a field on the morning of August 23, 1826; only one left the spot alive.

The word "duel," most likely an elision of the Latin *duellum* (war between two), entered the English language around the beginning of the seventeenth century. Single combat, of course, is as old as the hills where David slew Goliath but no laws regulating its conduct existed until the beginning of the sixth century, when King Gundebald of Burgundy decided that irreconcilable differences could be settled through trial by combat. Such confrontations, conducted before magistrate and public, became known as judicial duels. The duel of honor, on the other hand, was private, secular, and, for most of its history, illegal. It came about during the Italian Renaissance, when certain aristocrats, hoping to establish themselves as a social, as well as a military, class affected an exaggerated sense of honor. Dozens of duelling codes, fencing manuals, and treatises on courtesy soon materialized, prescribing the dress, manners, and rules of combat appropriate to the courtier. In effect, they provided the ground on which abstract notions of honor coalesced into the precepts and axioms that enabled a man of the upper class to live a more noble life. Such a man would keep his word, rush to the aid of a comrade or a woman in distress, and never allow an insult or injury to himself or his family to go unavenged.

Shaped by the codes duello, the Italian duel was an elaborate performance in which civility and justice played equal
parts. A courtier entered into a duel not to kill his opponent
but to reestablish his honor, his sword a symbolic prop until
the moment it was drawn. In fact, so long as the *puntiglio
d'onore* was observed, the outcome of the duel was irrelevant.
As the historian Donald Weinstein remarked, "The duel imagined (and avoided) was as real and as serious as the duel
fought." Interestingly, a challenge did not always lead to a
confrontation. Loopholes and precautions were built into the
codes, allowing for a cooling-off period in which the seconds
could try to negotiate a peace. The codes also contained
detailed instructions for the writing of letters, or cartels,
which spelled out the exact nature of the offense and the ways
to respond to it. Some Italian gentlemen, apparently, became
so fixated on the rules—splitting hairs over some minor point
of honor and writing to one another about it—that they never
got around to the duel itself.

From Italy, the duel of honor spread to France and then
the rest of Europe. Fifty years after Baldassare Castiglione's
Book of the Courtier (1528) informed men of rank that their
"first duty" was to become acquainted with every kind of
weapon, the French were making Italians look like stragglers.
Not only did the king's minions fillet each other at the drop of
a plumed hat, their seconds and thirds often joined in with
what the sixteenth-century writer Pierre Brantôme described
as *"gaîté de coeur."* Although English gentlemen did not duel
with the fervor of their French counterparts, duelling
remained a good career move in Britain into the early nineteenth century.

The Irish, too, were redoubtable duellists, but so lacking in
decorum when potting each other that, in 1777, delegates from

five counties assembled to hammer out the Irish Code Duello. New duelling codes also appeared in France in 1836, in America in 1838, and in Prussia, and the Austro-Hungarian Empire around the start of the twentieth century. By then, the German duel had acquired a semi-mythic glow. German students could be found hacking at one another with a *Schläger*, a straight-edged sword whose abbreviated point, while not lethal, inflicted "bragging scars." The student duel, known as *die Mensur*, was an approved pedagogical exercise, a preparatory step toward the all-important duel of honor. Kevin McAleer, the author of *Dueling: The Cult of Honor in Fin-de-Siècle Germany* (1994), contends that duelling was an attempt to recover "an illusory German past in which men of honor righted all manner of wrong with a single stroke of the winking blade." For generations of German plutocrats, duelling was a bastion against weakness, effeminacy, and decadence. Even Theodor Herzl, one of the first advocates of Zionism, couldn't help thinking that "a half dozen duels would very much raise the social position of the Jews."

Although duelling began with the admirable goal of curbing, or at least regulating, impromptu sword fights, it rarely met with official favor. As early as 1480, Isabella of Spain banned it, as did subsequent Spanish, French, German, and English monarchs. The Church consistently condemned it, and, in 1563, the Council of Trent decreed that all duellists were to be excommunicated. Anti-duelling legislation, however, proved remarkably ineffective. Kings were reluctant to punish the wayward nobles who supplied the men for their armies, and the courts were not much better. Despite legal rulings mandating heavy fines, imprisonment, and even execution, tolerance generally prevailed, probably because intolerance wouldn't have made much difference.

A gentleman duelled to show that he could—to confirm his standing in society and to demonstrate that honor trumped both God and king. Putting an end to the practice would have required not just a ban but the dismantling of the idealistic framework that supported it. After becoming Lord Protector in 1653, Oliver Cromwell quickly issued a proclamation against duelling and also—according to Jonathan Swift, who had it on good authority—strongly encouraged his nobles to adopt a rude and jokey familiarity with one another. Phony insults, he hoped, would inure them to real ones.

James Landale seems to have missed Cromwell's cunning little scheme, but he hasn't missed much else. In rounding out his story, he has looked in all the right places and all the right books, from Andrew Steinmetz's pioneering *The Romance of Duelling in All Times and Countries* (1868) to V. G. Kiernan's magisterial, if somewhat Marxist-tinged, *The Duel in European History* (1986). The duel between David Landale and George Morgan figures in neither of these books, nor does it rate a mention in Robert Baldick's anecdotal standby *The Duel* (1965) or in Barbara Holland's more recent *Gentleman's Blood* (2003). But then Landale and Morgan weren't exactly gallants vying for the same woman. One was a merchant, the other a banker; and the initial cause of dispute was a refusal of credit. Taken aback by Morgan's decision not to honor a bill of exchange, Landale, understandably, took his business elsewhere. Morgan, out of spite, then spread rumors about Landale's financial stability, which prompted Landale to write an indignant letter to the Bank of Scotland. Infuriated, Morgan then went out of his way to provoke a challenge.

Like Hamilton before him, David Landale was maneuvered into a duel by a sensitivity to honor's dictates. Failing to issue a challenge when provoked, according to "The British Code of Duel" of 1824, was as dishonorable as failing to answer one. Nominally, it was Landale's "call," but it was Morgan who, by undermining Landale's reputation—not to mention hitting him with an umbrella—made the duel inevitable. Perhaps the most affecting element of James Landale's *The Last Duel* is its measured account of how peaceable men living ordinary lives, whose worlds were circumscribed by the flow of business transactions and church functions, could be ensnared by the concept of honor and forced into a situation where extreme violence was meted out with extreme politeness.

This was not what the framers of the first duelling codes had intended. They assumed that, by classifying offenses and prescribing appropriate punishments, they would make men think twice about resorting to violence. The duel of honor was supposed to cut back on unchecked violence—on the assassinations, vendettas, and unruly affrays (where dozens of men rushed at one another with broadswords and axes) that were rife in the Middle Ages. The gentry, however, took honor so seriously that just about every offense became an offense against honor. Two Englishmen duelled because their dogs had fought. Two Italian gentlemen fell out over the respective merits of Tasso and Ariosto, an argument that ended when one combatant, mortally wounded, admitted that he had not read the poet he was championing. And Byron's great-uncle William, the fifth Baron Byron, killed a man after disagreeing about whose property furnished more game. As for the seconds, whose stated role was to reconcile potential opponents, it's impossible to know how many duels they averted, but a hint may be found in the words of an Italian fencing master: "It is not the sword or the pistol that kills, but the seconds."

Thus, an institution devised as a way of regulating violence became a spur to violence. In France, during the reign of Henry IV, at least four thousand men died in private combat. (One source puts that number at an astonishing ten thousand.) Honor may have been the stated pretext for fighting, but some men, it seemed, just needed the action. Courtiers duelled to show off the *passado* (forward thrust) *or punto reverso* (backhand thrust), or they duelled to impress a princess, eliminate a rival, or curry favor with a higher-up. Instead of arguments leading to a duel, the duel became a reason to have an argument. One French nobleman simply sent a card to his neighbors that read, "I have reduced your house to ashes, ravished your wife, and hanged your children. Your mortal enemy, Lagarde."

If honor made some men touchy, duelling over trifles made honorable men uneasy. Sir Walter Raleigh thought duelling much too serious to be engaged in casually, and, in a single sentence, managed to link honor, reputation, and regard for the duel with concerns about its abuse: "It is an extreme rudeness to tax any man in public with an untruth . . . but all that is rude ought not to be civilized with death." Yet, despite its excesses, the duel remained for centuries a valid means to redress a wrong. For one thing, the sword was quicker and more binding than the gavel—a man who'd been cheated in a business deal might prefer to issue a challenge than engage in tedious, convoluted legal proceedings. Then, too, some offenses seemed to cry out for personal attention. "A man may shoot the man who invades his character, as he may shoot him who attempts to break into his house," Samuel Johnson trumpeted.

But even in those cases where the offense was egregious and retribution automatic, a paradox snaked its way around the duelling codes: by classifying what constituted an offense, they multiplied the opportunities for men to kill each other. So, did the duel check insolence and incivility? Or did it simply give men license to indulge in aggressive behavior? It probably did both—which is why reasonable men both defended and deplored it. Sydney Smith, the nineteenth-century clergyman and wit, summed up the ambivalence: "Duelling, though barbarous in civilized [people], is a highly civilized institution among barbarous people, and when compared to assassination, is a prodigious victory gained over human passions."

Four hundred years ago, Francis Bacon suggested that duelling would disappear as it made its way down the social ladder. The aristocracy, he told the Star Chamber, would disdain the duel once it was taken up by "Barbers-surgeons and Butchers, and such base mechanicall persons." But the duel didn't die out; only the fashionable duel did. With Europe undergoing continuous wars from 1792 to 1815, armies became self-enclosed societies that increasingly played by their own rules. The British Army, in particular, became home to aristocrats short of money and a middle class that felt shortchanged by not being upper class. The former brought with it the duelling ethos, and the latter bought into it. Newly minted officers immediately began challenging one another in order to gain the honor of having fought a duel.

One beneficiary of rank, James Landale writes, was his ancestor's tormentor George Morgan. In 1812, Morgan had managed to purchase a commission in the 45th Regiment of Foot. He saw action in the Peninsular War in Spain, and, after being demobbed, never let anyone forget the service he'd rendered to His Majesty. In spite of this, David Landale felt obliged to ask his friends whether Morgan was even worthy of a duel. Landale was deceiving himself: the honor at the heart of duelling codes was a matter of indifference to men who used the duel as a step up. Pistols had made fencing lessons and a coat of arms superfluous, and anyone capable of cocking a hammer and pulling a trigger was now fit to duel.

Pistols lowered the tone, not just because of their owners' status but because they didn't shoot straight. They misfired; they exploded in the hand; they killed people standing nearby; and they inspired such quaint variations as the duel *au mouchoir*, in which duellists stood close enough to hold opposite corners of a handkerchief. Eventually, as guns were made safer and more accurate, the pistol duel came to be seen as fairer than a sword fight. The English, however, couldn't resist taking fairness to yet another level. Wouldn't the duel be more sporting if, say, the adversaries didn't actually aim? Perhaps because Landale and Morgan were Scottish, or because the malevolence of one was matched by the grim fatalism of the other, both men sighted down the barrels of their guns and fired simultaneously. For what seemed like ten seconds to one witness, the two men remained standing; then Morgan "gently fell on his right side." He died without uttering a word.

For James Landale, the consternation occasioned by Morgan's death and the ensuing trial of David Landale attest to the waning popularity of the duel. Landale is right to point out that fewer duels were being fought in Britain as the century wore on; nonetheless, there still seemed little reason *not* to duel if one were so inclined. By 1844, Queen Victoria had had enough. At her urging, the articles of war were amended to read that any officer involved in a duel, or with knowledge of one, would be cashiered out of the army. A year later, Prime

Minister Robert Peel (who, earlier in his career, had famously challenged the Irish nationalist Daniel O'Connell) added the clincher: widows of officers killed in a duel would not receive a pension. Moral obligation had shifted from personal honor to communal concern. The duellist came to be viewed as someone who cared more about himself than his family or country, and, for the first time, there existed a manifestly honorable reason not to fight.

Meanwhile–on the Continent and in the American South— men dueled with abandon. The Prussian Law Code of 1794, although it forbade duelling, managed to enhance its social prestige by discriminating among duellists; duels not conducted by officers or nobility were simply judged as assault or murder. The Germans then went at it with solemn menace, ceasing only when the kaiser or a superior officer commanded them to. (Apparently, the only thing more dishonorable than not duelling was not following orders.) By the end of the nineteenth century, Germans were fighting fewer duels than the French, but their mortality rate was higher. While a Frenchman still insisted on the right to duel, a touch on the arm with a sword, or a pistol shot that went noticeably wide, was often enough to satisfy honor. The French duel had, in fact, become something of a dog-and-pony show, where onlookers could anticipate a frisson, but not a funeral. Mark Twain, visiting Europe in the eighteen-seventies, reported that during a pistol duel each man's gallery, for its own safety, was positioned directly behind the duellist.

Five hundred years after the formulation of the original honor codes, the duel still engaged men in society, the military, and government. Europeans were duelling after the invention of the telephone, after cars started coming off assembly lines, after Einstein published his special theory of relativity. Despite growing moral disapprobation, men seemed unwilling to relinquish their right to duel; and the anti-duelling leagues that arose toward the end of the nineteenth century only attested to the duel's resilience. Tolstoy underscored its ethical slipperiness when, late in life, he mused that he had "killed men in war, and challenged men to duels in order to kill them . . . yet people saw nothing amiss."

Had Tolstoy, who died in 1910, lived another ten years, he would have seen duelling begin to dwindle in Europe. It's not that a banner of common sense had unfurled over the Continent but, rather, that the First World War brought about a profound sense of change. The enormous number of deaths, and the appalling waste and devastation, led to an abiding cynicism about the cultural values—including honor—that had characterized the pre-1914 moral landscape. Ideas about democratization and modernization may have cast duelling in a slightly ridiculous light, but it was the historical disconnect with the past that firmly relegated the duel to another age and another state of mind. V. G. Kiernan, in his history of the European duel, viewed the First World War as, among other things, "a duel that virtually ended duelling." There was also a more corporeal reason for the decline of the duel: an entire generation of potential duellists in France, Germany, and England—those honor-bound officers who led their men in the trenches—had been all but wiped out.

Perhaps it was inevitable, then, that duelling, which most of Europe and the American South had associated with chivalrous deeds, soon came to represent a distant and better world. The Austrian writer Arthur Schnitzler, who had opposed duelling for much of his career, recalled it wistfully in a short story written after the war: "Life was more beautiful, and in any case, offered a nobler vision then." A duel, Schnitzler's narrator concedes, may have been over something trivial, but dying for the "emptiness" of honor was surely preferable to "dying for much less and to no purpose, upon the command or wish of other people." At least those who duelled had "a certain bearing," which the horrors of war had utterly destroyed.

Schnitzler knew that he was addressing a phantom. Life may have seemed more beautiful before, but, in reality, the only thing beautiful about a duel was the spot where it might take place: a leafy glade in the Bois de Boulogne, or a snow-laden field along the Rhine. Duels were a bloody business, often concluding with a piece of sharp steel piercing the body, or a bullet plowing through tissue and bone. Men not killed outright could die in great pain from ruptured organs and suppurating infections. But one can't blame writers for adding to the duel's mystique. The duel, after all, lends itself to drama, character study, suspense, and a heightened dénouement. Sir Walter Scott and Alexandre Dumas père made it a staple of their novels, and memorable duels occur in the work of Maupassant, Pushkin, Conrad, Lermontov, Tolstoy, Chekhov, and Thomas Mann. A duel also makes a great painterly tableau, stark and eerily beautiful. Ritual, however, should not be confused with beauty. The formal nature of the duel may have lent it a patina of civility, but it didn't make duelling any less violent. Good posture only makes you appear taller.

The history of the duel is one of increasingly shabby ironies. Established to help a burgeoning aristocracy distinguish itself from mere soldiery, the duel becomes, at one point, almost completely martial. Zealously guarded by marginalized aristocrats, who saw it as an exclusive right, the duel evolves, with the improvement of sidearms, into a decidedly middle-class pursuit. And, finally, honor itself, once capable of being described as "an instinct of incomparable beauty," is unable to survive the uses to which men had put it. Honor? Honor is the leader of a street gang who won't be dissed; it is a Mafia capo on "The Sopranos" who demands satisfaction when his fat wife is called fat; and, in the ultimate perversion, it is the slogan on the belt buckle of Himmler's S.S. troops—"My Honor Is Loyalty."[2]

Men—especially young men—have always taken each other's measure and gotten in each other's face. In the days when knighthood was in flower, bored aristocrats devised a form of combat known as *pas d'armes*, where one knight carved out some imagined territory for himself and then dared another knight to cross it. Fans of *Monty Python and the Holy Grail* may recall John Cleese rapidly losing his limbs while refusing to budge from his self-appointed estate. Silly stuff – but how is it different from the story of the two British officers stationed in India, who, on being denied the use of weapons to settle a dispute, agreed to enter a dark room in which a venomous snake lay coiled?

Honor may still have one more side to it. If the Y chromosome chafes at being disrespected and bullied, it probably has little to do with honor and everything to do, according to

[2] James Bowman's *Honor: A History* does an excellent job of tracing honor's bumpy departure from Western culture. The dismissal of honor—a result of the intellectual currents swirling around pacifism, psychotherapy, and feminism—has, in Bowman's opinion, left us without an ethical bulwark. Instead of borrowing selectively from what was good from an older culture, we have established an "anti-honor liberalism" incapable of recognizing and dealing with cultures where the concept of honor—however perverted—continues to hold sway.

evolutionary biologists, with atavistic competition for wealth and power and the chance to reproduce. But perhaps we fight, too, because we can't risk being perceived as weak. Whatever else "honor" may be, it is the knowledge that every impertinence carries with it the seed of a greater, more fundamental insult: the suggestion that a person can *get away* with it— which is, after all, where humiliation really begins.

Somewhere in our molecular makeup a sword-bearing protein squalls to have its day. But that doesn't mean we have to listen. Although there are occasions that justify armed combat, a challenge to a duel isn't one of them. Life is short and dangerous enough—why lower the odds of survival, why make existence even more precarious? "My friend, let us speak frankly," Schnitzler wrote, apropos of the duel, "one must be somewhat limited to stare death so calmly in the face." Ultimately, the duel was sustained not by a failure of communication but by a failure of imagination. Our duelling days are over now, but, as we look around, it appears that the collective imagination has still not grasped the prophecy of cut steel, the secret germinating inside the barrel of a gun.

8

SOME REMARKS ON THE PITFALLS OF BIOGRAPHY

Especially Where Writers are Concerned

Biographies bore me. The more "definitive" the biography, the more hopelessly bored I become. Perhaps I should qualify this. Not *all* biographies bore me, but there's an excellent chance that a book about a writer, especially one bursting at the seams with the fussy details of everyday life, will function as a sleep aid. I may not subscribe to F. Scott Fitzgerald's dictum that a good novelist is too many people for a biographer to pin down, but I do contend that books about literary figures are usually less interesting than those about people who actually make things happen. There's nothing unusual or belittling about this. After all, the lives of certain people—explorers, robber barons, athletes, military, religious, and political leaders, or particularly rambunctious painters—are filled with conflict and competition, which naturally tend to enliven narratives about them.

But writers, so to speak, are another story. Their struggles are mainly internal and most of them end up spending too much time at their desks to lead adventurous lives. Yes, there are exceptions—Dickens, Dostoevsky, Hemingway, and Fitzgerald had some wild rides between books—but the exploits of most novelists usually occur between their ears. As a result, their lives are generally no more compelling than anyone else's, and possibly less so. The fact that a writer has produced an important body of work does not necessarily justify a voluminous biography. Henry James was, to say the least, an interesting man (had an interesting family, too, I hear), but are *five* hefty volumes necessary to reconstitute his life? Leon Edel evidently thought so, but I suspect that after working tirelessly to uncover every detail of James's life, he could not bear to part with *anything* he had learned.

Admittedly, not every large, full-scale biography of a writer is unreadable. Who could deny the pleasures contained in such splendid works as Richard Ellman's *Oscar Wilde*, Leslie Marchand's *Byron*, or Michael Holroyd's *George Bernard Shaw*, each of them heavier than a newborn tiger cub. Indeed, some biographies require amplitude, especially when the author has something more in mind than simply "A Life of." A biography may substitute as cultural history, as is the case with Jacques Barzun's two-volume *Berlioz and the Romantic Century* and Joseph Frank's five-volume *Dostoevsky*, books that not only offer a gloss on just about everything that Berlioz and Dostoevsky composed but constitute intellectual histories of nineteenth-century Europe.

Still, if I were forced to choose between a hulking book or a well-shaped essay about a novelist, I would choose the essay every time. The great majority of writers—even such wonderful writers as John Cheever and J. D. Salinger—simply don't require that many pages devoted to them. I have a soft spot for John Clare, but I'm pretty sure that a two-hundred-page book about him would try my patience. (Jonathan Bates's six-hundred page biography of Clare, good as it is, makes my point.) Perhaps I'm being unfair, but whenever I glance at one of those "magesterial" studies of poets, I find it to be over-blown and prolix, simultaneously cluttered and windy. Give me instead a medium-size book like Hesketh Pearson's *The Smith of Smiths* or a well-written entry in a *Famous Lives* series, something I can finish between Christmas and Lent.

It all began, of course, with Boswell's *The Life of Samuel Johnson*. Whatever one thinks of Boswell's book, it's a biography in name only. Mostly, it's smart, entertaining table-talk. Boswell, who encountered Johnson when the older man was fifty-three, chose to concentrate on the six months they spent together rather than on Johnson's formative years. And per-haps because Boswell's *Johnson* is one *Life* that actually needs fleshing out, subsequent biographers of Johnson, and of prac-tically everyone else, have made sure to leave nothing out, no matter how trivial. In such cases, scholarship, I'm sorry to say, is just another name for bloat.

Johnson was lucky. The biographies at *his* disposal were relatively brief and concerned themselves with the great fig-ures of the past: Vasari's *Lives of the Artists*, Dryden's transla-tion of Plutarch's *Lives*, Thomas Fuller's *The History of the Worthies of England*. In 1750 Johnson could look around and propose that "no species of writing seems more worthy of cul-tivation than biography, since none can be more delightful or more useful, none can more certainly enchain the heart by irresistible interest, or more widely diffuse instruction to every diversity of condition." Still, the Great Age of Biogra-phy, as it's sometimes called, didn't emerge until the latter part of the eighteenth century, nicely exemplified by Johnson's own *Critical Lives of the Poets*. So popular did the genre become that, in 1832, Benjamin Disraeli took a moment in one of his novels to advise readers: "Rise early and regularly, and read for three hours. Read the Memoirs of the Cardinal de Retz, the Life of Richelieu, everything about Napoleon—read works of that kind . . . Read no history: nothing but biography, for that is life without theory. Then fence."

Disraeli might have distinguished between biography and history, but Emerson was less rigorous. "All history resolves itself very easily into the biography of a few stout and earnest persons," Emerson declared, which practically made the genre de rigueur in humanities courses; and for a time the difference between popular and scholarly biographies was not as great as one might think. But in the second quarter of the last century, history departments began to discard the Great Man or World Historical Figure in favor of material conditions and states of mind. Instead of books about individuals bestriding events, we got books in which events derived from the customs and behaviors of regional people, whose history was determined by unique configurations of economic, social, and geographic forces.

Literature, too, became both more technical and more historically conditioned. In fact, one could say that the study of literature bifurcated into the aesthetic and the social. While the New Critics dismissed biography as a means of understanding a writer's work (if one wished to practice criticism, one examined the work as an autonomous text, independent of the person who created it), Marxist critics regarded the work as evidence of the class struggle, an inevitable byproduct of social and economic pressures. In any event, while the public's appetite for old-fashioned biographies remained undiminished, the genre as a tool of literary criticism fell into disuse.

Until now. Biography has, it seems, returned to the university in the guise of "life-writing," a term that effectively wastes two good words. Apparently, the existential nature of the biographic impulse puts the finished product in the same category as memoirs, letters, diaries, essays, blogs, and e-mails. So one might infer from The Centre for Life History and Life Writing Research at the University of Sussex. Biography, of course, deviates from other forms of life-writing in that it is one life writing about another, which seems necessary to say only because biography is also seen to be "a contested space." What this means is that biography, like all written discourse, serves different masters, each of whom answers to a higher law, that of cultural context. And what *this* means is that a biography—whether it's hagiographic or iconoclastic—is necessarily embedded in the culture of its day.

Fair enough, but what, finally, is the point of knowing that mind and language are subject to the social and psychological circumstances that formed them? If even the methods we use to reject culture are culturally determined, then an infinite and rather tiresome regress begins to color all intellectual effort. Moreover, there is nothing profound or revelatory in claiming that cultural bias informs the biographical enterprise. Plutarch's *Lives* purposely compared Greek and Roman leaders; Hazlitt's *Spirit of the Age* didn't exactly pull any punches in scrutinizing dignitaries of the British Regency; and Lytton Strachey's *Eminent Victorians* plainly meant to influence as much as edify.

Leave it to W. H. Auden, however, to write a sonnet devoted to the biography:

> A shilling life will give you all the facts:
> How Father beat him, how he ran away,
> What were the struggles of his youth, what acts
> Made him the greatest figure of his day.

Auden's gentle reproof was not directed so much at the number of cheap biographies available, but at the idea that a life could be circumscribed by the *known* facts about it. A lesson, unfortunately, not taken to heart. Once biography was dismissed from the academy, writers who wanted to make an impression simply worked harder to uncover *all* the facts, as if the sheer abundance of materials would magically elucidate the entire man or woman.

Although I may grumble at what I consider to be the recital of pointless details, I do admit to feeling a certain sympathy for biographers faced with authors who haven't exactly led picaresque lives (more writers are like Emily Dickinson than Joseph Conrad). Whereas great men and women make their times interesting by virtue of living in them, writers, for the most part, do little to alter the course of events. And should these scribblers live in a relatively quiet period, so much the worse for the biographer. Conversely, a small but significant percentage of poets and novelists seemingly cry out for someone to tell their stories. Their families, their personalities, the personalities of their friends and enemies, their histories as well as the history of their times are mines rich in anecdotal lore. One would have to work hard to make a *Life* of Stendhal or Hazlitt or Dostoevsky or Wilde boring.

Nonetheless, one doesn't have to delve into every corner of someone's life to gain a better understanding of his or her mind. More information does not necessarily grant us more knowledge. And given the difficulty of getting to know another person, imagine the problems involved in getting to know a writer. Writers complicate matters enormously. For starters, there's everything they've ever written—books, memoirs, letters, essays, and possibly journals, diaries, and notebooks—as well as everything that's been written about them, including books, essays, articles, and other people's memoirs. Gossip usually fills the air and gallops across the page, some of it based on the impressions of people who met the author, some on the impressions of people who didn't but knew someone who did. Now add to this the writer's tendency to record every waking thought and transient mood and we begin to appreciate that the fierce opinions contained in letters, in diary entries, or in others' recollections, though deeply felt on a particular day, could have been forgotten a week or a year later.

Beware, then, the definitive biography that sanctifies our knowledge of its subject. If works of philosophy are, as Nietzsche thought, unintentional memoirs, then biographies, too, are shaped by the temperament and experiences of their authors. Biographers may not fool with the facts, but they do select what to include, what to emphasize, what to downplay. And just as a movie director can shoot a scene from various angles, lighting it to make the actor or location look good, a biographer can zoom in to record a reaction, pan out to show what else is going on, or abruptly end a shot before we know how to react to it.

For the sake of argument, let's assume that biography is, if not completely objective, then a more disinterested art than autobiography. After all, enough memoirists from Rousseau onward have been found to—shall we say?—shade the truth. Even when they're not deliberately lying or taking evasive action, they tend to conceal as much as reveal. Cagey writers, for instance, might adopt a tone of frank intimacy, inserting wry, self–deprecating comments in order to gain our trust. Or they may confess to a small sin in order to divert our attention from larger ones. Of course, such tactics may only reflect a desperate desire to appear interesting. Imagine a memoir that is both brutally honest *and* boring; no one wants that. So it's always wise to expect a little rhetorical sleight-of-hand from confessional writers who are looking to impress by whatever means available.

Biographers, however, are beholden to report "the earthly pilgrimage of a man," to use Carlyle's description. A fairly straightforward commission, it seems to me—but when is anything about the literary life straightforward? Even when literary biographies were part of the humanities curriculum, there was debate about their usefulness. One might refer to this as the Proust—Sainte-Beuve dispute. Charles Augustis Sainte-Beuve, the nineteenth-century critic ("a clever man with the temper of a turkey," a countryman once observed) maintained that readers had to be familiar with a writer's life before they could understand his work. This attitude did not sit well with Proust, whose little book *contra Sainte-Beuve* hints at a different point of view. For Proust, a poem or novel does not hinge upon or even necessarily refer to the events of one's life, but proceeds from *l'autre moi*—i.e., the self who creates as opposed to the self who makes love, eats dinner, and writes letters. Literary biographers, you will be shocked to discover, lean heavily toward Monsieur Saint-Beuve. And though I'm not sure that Proust is entirely correct, I am sure that knowing every single detail of a writer's personal history will not add to my appreciation of the work.

I admit to a prejudice here. If we're talking about public figures who deliberately fashion personas in order to further their careers, I don't mind hearing about their moral failings and sexual pecccadilloes. But where literary figures are concerned, I prefer not to know. Serious writers—with the exception of Truman Capote and Norman Mailer, who deliberately made public spectacles of themselves—work in private, and their privacy ought to be respected. If our great writers must have flaws, let them be magnificent ones: an excess of pride or passion or commitment to a foolish cause. Let their faults be like cracks in the earth rather than hairline fractures along the rim of a Sevres teacup.

There was a time when canonical writers occupied a special place in the world of letters, when their spiritual and moral authority was so pervasive that readers were buoyed by their very existence. Such writers—Shakespeare, Hugo, Dickens, Tolstoy—seemed to understand human nature in all its astonishing complexity, and their works seemed to forgive humanity its mishaps and weaknesses. Reading them one no longer felt alone in the world; instead one sensed a compassionate intelligence that, while not countenancing all behavior, understood the reasons for it. "I am not an orphan on the earth, so long as this man lives on it," Maxim Gorky said to himself on first meeting Tolstoy.

But that, as they say, was in another country. And besides those writers are dead. Today, the invasive practices of journalism allot to every hero a few million valets, thereby preventing writers from attaining the authority that their predecessors were able to command. Perhaps it's naïve to believe that great writers make good fathers or mothers or that they practice flawless hygiene—but that's how I like to think of them. I'm not suggesting that we overlook T. S. Eliot's anti-Semitism or F. Scott Fitzgerald's racism; I'm saying that in terms of the work, a writer's biases and bad behavior are significant, but only up to a point.

The sad thing is, the keyhole approach to biography does occasionally shed light on some aspect of character. The question we have to ask, though, is: What's gained compared to what's lost? Even if a dark secret emerges from the shadows, or some behind-the-scenes shenanigans take center stage, do such discoveries enhance our knowledge of the work? Does this new-found information, bruited in newspapers and journals, make the work more brilliant, more powerful? Does it help us to understand a writer's genius? I would argue no.

Not everything about a writer's life is pertinent to the work; sometimes the more we know the less capable we are of seeing the work as the writer intended. Moral qualms, for example, may influence our response to certain scenes or characters because we happen to know something "shameful" or "weird" about the author. To which I say: Whatever traits Proust shared with the Baron de Charlus ought to remain between them. Frankly, I don't want to know. I wish I *didn't* know that Kafka kept a cache of porn, that Hemingway's mother dressed him as a girl and called him "Ernestine," that J. D. Salinger, according to his daughter, drank his own urine and sat for hours in an orgone box. Truthfully, I don't care how many boys Byron buggered or how many times a day Cheever masturbated. Simply because someone wrote good novels or poems does not entitle us to invade his or her privacy.

I myself am hardly blameless in this regard since in a book about Fitzgerald I quote from his letters to reinforce whatever points need discussing. Nonetheless, I would gladly sacrifice such insights. In fact, if it were up to me, I would discourage private letters from ever seeing the light of day—the letters, for example, between Scott and Zelda. Not all the letters, but certainly those written after Zelda's nervous breakdown in

1930, containing bitter recriminations and poignant reminders of happier days. These letters were not meant to be seen by anyone but their recipients. How do we in good conscience condone reading a letter that begins "Dearest Do Do"? Surely, Zelda still has an expectation of privacy that death cannot retract.

I am aware that my opinion goes counter to the prevailing temper, and I am willing to go even further. I would prohibit the publishing of diaries and journals containing information the author did not intend for public consumption. In an ideal world, scholars would retain the right to quote parts of the diaries or apprize us of their contents, but any wholesale reproduction of the pages would be forbidden by law (and censorship be damned). If nothing else, this might restrict the size and number of biographies.

Biography can be used for good or ill, and literary biography is no exception. In 1849, a peripheral literary man with the matinee-villain name of Rufus A. Griswold wrote a sketchy *Memoir of the Author*, which effectively trashed Edgar Allan Poe's good name for the next half century. George Eliot suffered a gentler decline in reputation after her death in 1880 because of the well-intentioned biography by her husband John Walter Cross. "It is not a Life at all," said William Gladstone. "It is a Reticence in three volumes." It required Virginia Woolf's appreciative essay in the *Times Literary Supplement* in 1920 to launch what has practically become a cottage industry. Not a decade now passes without a biography of Mary Ann Evans. Even *Moby Dick* was just an obscure novel by an unknown writer until Raymond Weaver's 1921 biography *Herman Melville: Man, Mariner and Mystic* began "The Melville Revival." As for F. Scott Fitzgerald, he—perhaps more than any other novelist—needed a biography to restore his reputation. *Gatsby*, in fact, didn't become great in the eyes of the general public until the 1950s with the publication of *The Far Side of Paradise*, Arthur Mizener's sympathetic biography of the author.

I suspect we haven't seen the last biography of Fitzgerald or George Eliot, just as we haven't seen the end of books about Virginia Woolf or Sylvia Plath, to name two more objects of biographic lust. Famous novelists will always attract biographers, since fame summons a large and loyal following willing to throw money at books about its favorite authors. Numbers, however, have a drawback: The more books there are about a person, the harder the next biographer must work to say something new; and whether a book is geared for one's colleagues or the general public, the urge to ferret out secrets, expose politically incorrect behavior, or dig up hitherto unknown bad acts, remains irresistible to all but the most judicious of researchers.

If biography is to some extent informed bias, that doesn't mean that the biographer is necessarily being unfair. There are some writers—not many, to be sure—whose lives are so complicated and whose personalities are so combustible that biographers almost reflexively narrow their focus in order to produce a coherent narrative. Perhaps every good novelist is, as Fitzgerald pointed out, many different people. But even if he's just two or three people, that's enough to make life difficult for the biographer. As Auden knew, there is something elusive and perhaps enigmatic about all of us, which precludes a complete and disinterested accounting. Something— we may not know what—will remain unknown. And this is where I part company with Sir Thomas Browne. I don't believe we *can* know "What song the Syrens sang, or the name

Achilles assumed when he hid himself among women." And I'm content to have it so. Each of us, I venture, moves along a different psychic current, each of us a unique amalgam of inherited and acquired characteristics. The most we can glean are partial views, glimmerings of another consciousness alone in a universe that occasionally brushes up against our own. "No one nature can extend entirely inside another," Fitzgerald observed.

Shortly before he died in December 1944, Fitzgerald jotted down a few lines of a poem.

> Your books were in your desk
>> I guess and some unfinished
>> Chaos in your head
> Was dumped to nothing by the great janitress
>> Of destinies.

For Fitzgerald's sake, let's hope that he would have changed or excised the last two lines. As for the other fifteen words, they suggest the intense self-awareness typical of all writers, from the most sensible and down-to-earth to the most sensive and volatile—all have some unfinished chaos in their heads. Now all the dutiful biographer has to do is identify, arrange, and pin that chaos to the page. What could be simpler?

9

SLOW FADE

F. Scott Fitzgerald in Hollywood

"Dear Scott: I don't know where you are living and I'll be damned if I believe anyone lives in a place called 'The Garden of Allah,'" Thomas Wolfe wrote to F. Scott Fitzgerald, in July of 1937. Wolfe sent his letter "c/o Charles Scribner's Sons," knowing that their editor, Maxwell Perkins, would forward it to Fitzgerald wherever he might be. Fitzgerald was, in fact, living at the Garden of Allah, a bungalow colony on Sunset Boulevard in Hollywood, along with Dorothy Parker, Robert Benchley, S. J. Perelman, Ogden Nash, and other writers in the screen trade. He had arrived earlier that month to take a job at the MGM studio in Culver City. He occupied a small office on the third floor of the writers' building, where from ten in the morning until six at night he worked on scripts and drank bottles of Coca-Cola, carefully arranging the empties around the room. Fitzgerald lasted eighteen months at MGM, during which time he worked on five scripts, wrote another one more or less from scratch, and generated a pile of notes and memos. And if his work was altered or rejected, he'd follow up with bitter, self-justifying letters.

There was a spate of such letters. Fitzgerald, to put it mildly, did not impress the studio bosses. The rap against him was that he couldn't make the shift from words on the page to images on the screen. His plotting was elaborate without purpose; his dialogue arch or sentimental; and his tone too serious—at times, even grim. Billy Wilder, who seemed genuinely fond of Fitzgerald, likened him to "a great sculptor who is hired to do a plumbing job"—with no idea how to connect the pipes and make the water flow.

On the face of it, he should have taken Hollywood by storm: he wrote commercially successful stories; he knew how to frame a scene; and his dialogue, at least in his best fiction, was smart, sophisticated, evocative. And of all the American novelists writing in the 1920s and '30s—Dreiser, Lewis, Hemingway, Dos Passos, Steinbeck—Fitzgerald had the strongest attachment to Hollywood. As a boy, he was a passionate moviegoer; he directed and acted in plays, and his desk was filled, he later recalled, with "dozens of notebooks containing the germs of dozens of musical comedies." Moreover, three of his early stories had been made into silent films, as had his novels *The Beautiful and Damned* and *The Great Gatsby*. Fitzgerald began trying to write for the movies as early as 1922, and yet, for all his efforts, he earned exactly one screen credit: a shared billing on *Three Comrades*. So what was the problem?

Five years ago, Fitzgerald's Hollywood career came in for a new round of scrutiny, when the University of South Carolina paid $475,000 for the bulk of his MGM output. The material had gathered dust in the MGM archives until an employee named Martin Kraegel salvaged it in the early Seventies, when the company began to consolidate its assets. Kraegel then sat on the documents (around two thousand pages, some in penciled longhand) for another three decades before attempting to sell them. But there was a complication. Strictly speaking, he didn't own the papers; at any rate, he didn't own the intellectual rights to them. Nor, as it turned out, did the Fitzgerald estate. Lawyers determined that, since the manuscripts had been generated as "work for hire," such rights belonged to Time Warner, which had bought Turner Broadcasting System in 1996, which, in turn, had owned MGM's film library since 1986.

Enter Matthew J. Bruccoli, industrious collector of all things Fitzgeraldian, who, for nearly forty years, until his death in 2008, taught at the University of South Carolina. Bruccoli authenticated the papers and, in April, 2004, helped broker a deal bringing them to the university, where— christened the "Warner Bros./Turner Entertainment F. Scott Fitzgerald Screenplay Collection"—they reside in the Thomas Cooper Library.

Although a number of writers have addressed Fitzgerald's time in Hollywood, his biographers have generally given short shrift to the screenplays—the assumption being that he wrote them for the money. You bet he did—as did Raymond Chandler, William Faulkner, Anthony Powell, P. G. Wodehouse, Aldous Huxley, and half a dozen other literary luminaries—but for Fitzgerald it wasn't just about the money. According to Charles Marquis Warren, Fitzgerald's collaborator on a screen treatment of *Tender Is the Night*, "Scott would rather have written a movie than the Bible, than a best-seller." This overstates the case, but Fitzgerald was certainly the first American novelist to take the movies seriously and the first to regard his own talent as a natural fit with Hollywood. One might also add that his life exemplified that all-too-neat reversal of fortune of which Hollywood studios were so fond.

No American writer before Fitzgerald had achieved success so young or fallen from favor quite so quickly. Born on September 24, 1896, in St. Paul, Minnesota, he entered Princeton University in 1913, but did not graduate; he joined the Army in 1917, but never made it overseas; and then, like Byron, nearly a century earlier, he awakened one morning to find himself famous. His first novel, *This Side of Paradise* (1920), featuring sensitive Ivy League students, struck a chord, when chords still vibrated to bobbed hair and petting. In the 1920s, he and his wife, the mercurial Zelda Sayre Fitzgerald, romped through the capitals of Europe, seemingly with a highball in either hand. The Twenties were Scott's decade, a moment when the nation, as he put it, "was going on the greatest, gaudiest spree in history." He dubbed that spree the Jazz Age, and he and Zelda were forever associated with its lavish parties, bathtub gin, and cloche-hatted flappers.

Part of our fascination with Fitzgerald involves his fall from grace. The Depression repudiated not only the Jazz Age but also the writer most associated with it. The man who commanded between three thousand and four thousand dollars for a short story as late as 1930 was forgotten by the reading public six years later; in 1936, his total book royalties amounted to just over eighty dollars. Money problems were the least of it. In the early thirties, his fourth attempt at a novel (about a cameraman who dreams of being a director), which eventually became *Tender Is the Night* (about a psychiatrist who behaves like a director), was giving him fits. He was drinking too much and popping pills both to sleep and to wake up. His marriage was deteriorating—Zelda suffered a mental breakdown in 1930, and was in and out of sanitariums for the rest of her life—and in November, 1935, he bolted to Hendersonville, North Carolina, where he took a room in a hotel and began writing three confessional articles for *Esquire* (posthumously included in *The Crack-Up*), which horrified his friends and further damaged his reputation. Finally, there was the disastrous interview he gave to the New York *Post*, on his fortieth birthday, which made him sound like a drunken, unstable has-been.

Hollywood was his last chance: if he could establish himself in the film industry, then maybe his health, his confidence, and his creative juices would return. Twice before he had made the trip west: the first time in 1927, when he considered himself "a sort of magician with words," and again, in 1931, when he was asked to adapt a popular novel of the day. Neither venture had panned out, and Fitzgerald returned east, feeling thwarted by studio bigwigs. Part of his problem with Hollywood had to do with the man he admired most in the industry: Irving Thalberg, the wunderkind who ran Universal City at the age of twenty-one, and MGM four years later. Thalberg was responsible for the assembly-line method of screenwriting—successive teams of writers tweaking the same story—which incensed Fitzgerald. Most writers, apart from a few script-savvy specialists like Ben Hecht and Anita Loos, were considered cogs in the machine, or, in Jack Warner's gracious phrase, "schmucks with Underwoods." Fitzgerald returned the compliment. "I hate the place like poison with a sincere hatred," he wrote to his agent, Harold Ober, in 1935. By 1937, however, adrift and miserable, he was desperate to return.

But Hollywood was in no hurry to have him back. It was only through the intercession of an old friend that MGM hired him—at a thousand dollars per week, for six months. Though he was, as he later put it, "a pretty broken and prematurely old man who hasn't a penny except what he can bring out of a weary mind and sick body," Fitzgerald boarded the train to Los Angeles with an optimistic step. He had a plan. Fitzgerald always had a plan. He liked to draw up schedules; he kept meticulous records; he made numerous lists; and he recorded every penny earned, borrowed, and paid back. For a man who led one of the messiest lives in literary history, on paper he was as organized as Felix Unger's sock drawer. "I must be very tactful but keep my hand on the wheel," he wrote to his daughter, Scottie, from the train. "Find out the key man among the bosses + the most malleable among the collaborators. Given a break I can make them double this contract in less than two years."

Despite his previous experiences, Fitzgerald still felt there must be a trick to writing a good screenplay. So he familiarized himself with the logistical bric-a-brac of camera movements, and watched popular films, like *A Star Is Born*, over and over, pinpointing every single shot, and typing up his findings, two columns per page, until he had seven pages of:

GROUP SHOT	MED. TWO SHOT
CLOSE UP	CLOSE SHOT
TWO SHOT	CLOSE SHOT
GROUP SHOT	CLOSE SHOT
CLOSE SHOT	CLOSE UP

I came across this singular inventory when I visited the Thomas Cooper Library at the University of South Carolina early in September. I wanted to see for myself what Fitzgerald had been up to in California, and, as I sat in a temperature-controlled room on the mezzanine floor, examining the documents liberated from MGM's basement, I discovered just how hard he had worked at his craft. Fitzgerald approached each assignment with an intensity that must have puzzled his superiors. Given a script to revise, he would break it down, back-story it, advise the producers of its potential, and then start to add layers. *A Yank at Oxford* couldn't be just an innocent romance; it had to probe the connection between language and mores. *Madame Curie* couldn't be just the story of a woman overcoming the odds; it had to reveal the intricacies of a marriage between equals. Naturally, he became emotionally invested in the work, making it difficult to cede control, and, like the British colonel in *The Bridge on the River Kwai*, he forgot that what he was building didn't belong to him, and, consequently, felt dismayed at its destruction.

Fitzgerald began his final screenwriting stint by writing "behind" another writer on *A Yank at Oxford*, or, as Meyer Wolfsheim would say, "Oggs-ford." At some point, two other writers took over and jettisoned much of his dialogue. He was then handed a screenplay-in-progress of Erich Maria Remarque's popular novel *Three Comrades*. After submitting his draft to Joseph Mankiewicz—who later produced *The Philadelphia Story* and wrote and directed *All About Eve*—he learned that he would be paired with a more experienced screenwriter. Disappointed, he resigned himself to a collaboration, and for five months the two men worked together, not always collegially, until they had a finished script. Mankiewicz, however, remained unimpressed, and decided to intervene. His changes horrified Fitzgerald, who shot off a letter:

> To say I'm disillusioned is putting it mildly. For nineteen years, with two years out for sickness, I've written best-selling entertainment, and my dialogue is supposedly right up at the top . . . I am utterly miserable at seeing months of

work and thought negated in one hasty week. I hope you're
big enough to take this letter as it's meant—a desperate
plea to restore the dialogue to its former quality . . . Oh, Joe,
can't producers ever be wrong? I'm a good writer—honest.

In 1938, *Three Comrades* was named one of the ten best
films of the year, but Fitzgerald took no pleasure in this. He
thought Mankiewicz a vulgarian who had traduced the spirit
of Remarque's novel and of *his* screenplay. Mankiewicz
shrugged off Fitzgerald's accusations. He even claimed never
to have received the pitiful letter. It was only decades later,
with the revival of critical interest in Fitzgerald, that Mankiewicz felt compelled to defend his actions. "I personally have
been attacked as if I had spat on the American flag because
it happened once that I rewrote some dialogue by F. Scott
Fitzgerald. But indeed it needed it! . . . It was very literary
dialogue, novelistic dialogue that lacked all the qualities
required for screen dialogue."

Despite Mankiewicz's retouchings, Fitzgerald's contract
was extended for a year and his salary rose to twelve hundred
and fifty dollars a week. "I am now considered a success in
Hollywood," he observed wryly, "because something which
I did not write is going on under my name, and something
which I did write has been quietly buried without any fuss or
row—not even a squeak from me. The change from regarding
this as a potential art to looking at it as a cynical business has
begun. But I still think that some time during my stay out
here I will be able to get something of my own on the screen
that I can ask my friends to see."

He thought that opportunity had arrived when he was
asked to write a script about adultery for Joan Crawford.
His screenplay *Infidelity* pleased neither his producer nor

the censorship office, and the project was shelved (though someone briefly thought it might fly if it were renamed *Fidelity*). He then worked on *Marie Antoinette*, followed by an adaptation of Clare Boothe Luce's *The Women*, neither of which he saw through to the end. He spent three months on *Madame Curie* (from a treatment by Aldous Huxley) and then, in early January, 1939, was lent out to David O. Selznick to polish *Gone with the Wind*. A week later, he was gone; MGM, meanwhile, without explanation, allowed his contract to lapse.

Fitzgerald initially resisted the idea that he was at fault. Somehow he managed to convince himself that screenwriting could be his métier and that he was capable of giving studio executives what they wanted. It was only toward the end of his life that he acknowledged that he "just couldn't make the grade as a hack— that, like everything else, requires a certain practiced excellence."

After leaving MGM, Fitzgerald went freelance, and was almost immediately teamed with the twenty-four-year-old screenwriter Budd Schulberg on a collegiate romance set during the annual Winter Carnival at Schulberg's alma mater, Dartmouth. Unfortunately, on the research trip east, Schulberg brought along two bottles of Mumm's for the flight, and by the time the two of them were over Kansas the writing was on the wall—which is to say that it never made it into a script. Fitzgerald drank practically the entire time they were in New York and Hanover and points in between; they were fired before they had even roughed out the story. Years later, Schulberg, who died in August 2009, recounted their hapless collaboration in his novel *The Disenchanted* and also in an *Esquire* article that portrayed Fitzgerald as "tired, sick, embattled, vain and proud and painfully conscious of his fall from fame and fortune and creative productivity."

During the spring of 1939, with the Dartmouth debacle weighing on him, Fitzgerald drank heavily, fought with his lover, the gossip columnist Sheilah Graham, and took a chaotic trip to Cuba with Zelda, where he was beaten up for trying to stop a cockfight. He spent a week on the David Niven vehicle *Raffles*, but, with no steady movie work, he began writing stories about a hack screenwriter named Pat Hobby. Then, one day in March, 1940, an independent producer by the name of Lester Cowan called him. Cowan had bought the rights to Fitzgerald's story *Babylon Revisited* and wanted Fitzgerald to turn it into a screenplay. Fitzgerald tailored the script, retitled *Cosmopolitan*, for Shirley Temple, and then spent an afternoon pitching the idea to her mother.

When word got out that Temple was considering *Cosmopolitan*, Fitzgerald's stock rose. Darryl Zanuck, at Twentieth Century Fox, hired him to revise a script of Emlyn Williams's play *The Light of Heart*. Buoyed by such interest, Fitzgerald began to refer to *Cosmopolitan* as his "great hope for attaining some real status as a movie man and not a novelist." "If I get a credit on either of these two last efforts," he wrote in October, 1940, "things will never again seem so black as they did a year ago when I felt that Hollywood had me down in its books as a ruined man—a label which I had done nothing to deserve." But Shirley Temple's mother dithered, and *Cosmopolitan* died, and, in November, Zanuck passed on his revision of *The Light of Heart*.

Students of Fitzgerald's Hollywood days, who insist on demonstrating his ineptness, inevitably fasten on a scene from his draft of *Three Comrades*. At one point, a young veteran, Bobby, places a call to a woman named Pat. As soon as Bobby recites the number, Fitzgerald cuts from his face to a celestial switchboard, where an angelic operator coos, "One moment, please—I'll connect you with heaven." We now cut to "St. Peter at the Pearly Gates, cackling: I think she's in." Back to: Bobby's face, "changing to human embarrassment," as Pat's voice says "Hello." An amusing conversation ensues between the awkward Bobby and the sophisticated Pat. We then cut to a satyr "who has replaced the angel at the switchboard, pulling out the plug with a sardonic expression." As the writer Tom Dardis observes, although such a sequence might work nicely in an Ernst Lubitsch comedy, it seems rather misguided in a story set in a grim post–First World War Germany.

Because Fitzgerald took his work seriously, his pedagogical instinct would invariably kick in and he would end up overwriting and overexplaining. Consider a setup from *Cosmopolitan*:

> 88. LONG SHOT—THE SHIP DOCKING—shooting from the angle of those waiting on the pier. Band music loud and spirited.

> 89. BEHIND THE PICKET BARRIER
> Pierre and Marion Petrie waiting in the crowd. He is a Frenchman with a military tradition that makes him pompous and ceremonious in his personality—but when he had taken off his uniform, back in 1919, it was apparent that nature had equipped him to be only a minor clerk.

"In 1919?" What sort of detail is that to put in a screenplay? Now follows a much longer, prosy summation of Marion Petrie's character and attitudes, all of which could be expressed in a few lines of dialogue instead of a paragraph or two:

His wife Marion . . . is an extremely pretty American woman of thirty-two who must have hoped for a better match. She is now in a state of great emotion—barely controlled. She is agitated almost to the breaking point by the news of her sister's suicide, which reached her last night in Paris. Always before this she has felt a certain secret jealousy of her sister, who has had great wealth and luxury.

Fitzgerald is not without his defenders. In *The Cinematic Vision of F. Scott Fitzgerald*, Wheeler Winston Dixon, a professor of film at the University of Nebraska, contends that Fitzgerald developed "an adroit and engagingly complex visual sensibility" based on fluid camera movement and astute intercutting. Dixon's case, however, rests entirely on *Infidelity*, which, admittedly, does emphasize the visual over the verbal. In fact, Fitzgerald went a little camera crazy with *Infidelity*. In his concern to register states of mind and the changing moods of a relationship, he has the camera constantly picking up and dropping off, trucking, panning, and shifting from a conventional two-shot to a P.O.V. shot. When two lovers suddenly realize they have been spotted, Fitzgerald insists that we see their reactions:

(Close-up of Iris: Her eyes look down, then look up again, then stare.

Two-shot of Iris and Nicolas. Nicolas looks up and sees Iris's expression. As he starts to turn and see what she is staring at, the camera drops them and pans very slowly around the room, including the sideboard, passing it and reaching the door.

Althea, motionless, stands in the doorway, regarding them. We are seeing her in a medium shot from their angle and we hold on it for a moment.

Two-shot of Nicolas and Iris from Althea's angle. Their
faces are shocked and staring.
Medium shot of Althea from their angle.

And so on for another half-dozen lines of instruction
before the parenthetical is complete. Although aspiring
screenwriters are admonished to "see it" before describing
it, they soon learn, if they're lucky enough to get a script produced, that no amount of visualization on their part guides a
director's framing of a scene. Fitzgerald certainly visualized
Infidelity, but, then again, his timing was sometimes off, and
the script, which was never finished, relies excessively on
flashbacks to convey a sense of what was lost. Fitzgerald
could figuratively wield the camera, but usually he had too
much to say to say it with a lens.

Fitzgerald wasn't naïve about the business; he knew that
movies were "a salaried affair and along architectural rather
than emotional lines." He also knew that screenwriting is an
opaque craft requiring clarification by cameras and actors.
Nevertheless, he couldn't overcome his aversion to its bare-
bones structure. When handed a script, he tackled it as a critic
or an editor rather than as a mechanic; he wanted to redesign
the car instead of just making it run better. The sad thing is, he
tried: he tried faithfully to give the studios what they wanted,
without quite realizing how short his attempts fell.

Every so often, though, he put together a sequence that you
know would work perfectly onscreen. There's a moment in
Cosmopolitan when Victoria, a girl of eleven, having sneaked
aboard a train heading for Switzerland, stumbles across a com-
partment occupied by a Circassian woman with three children.
When a Swiss official asks to see the woman's passport, the
mother "begins jabbering in obscure double-talk," and when he

turns his attention to Victoria, who doesn't have her passport, she "pretends to jabber, too, in a language exactly like theirs." In an instant, Fitzgerald establishes the young girl's smarts.

The difficulty in evaluating Fitzgerald as a screenwriter lies in the problematic nature of screenwriting itself. While really incompetent scripts are easy to spot, even a well-wrought screenplay is a poor predictor of either artistic or box-office success. A script is simply a blueprint, whose potential to be mediocre or brilliant lies outside the screenwriter's purview. You can't really tell what kind of tree will grow from the hundred-and-twenty-page acorn in your hands; too much depends on just about everything else—direction, cinematography, acting, music, editing. The unfinished nature of the form is, ultimately, what Fitzgerald could not abide. You can feel it in the prolixity of his scripts and in the dark grooves of his penciled notes: he wanted every screenplay to impart a moral lesson while illuminating the hidden facets of its characters.

Fitzgerald's scripts were hobbled by the same quality that lifted his fiction above the superficial: the complicated nature of his mind. He had started out thinking he had genius and a special destiny, and it was this belief in an ideal version of himself that, when transmuted into narrative form, won him both a wide audience and critical esteem. But that idealized self in all other respects eluded him, not because he drank too much or behaved badly but because he was a writer at war with his own inclinations. A self-professed "moralist at heart," he also wanted to be a hero and an entertainer. Goethe looked out from one eye; Lorenz Hart from the other. Although he came to believe that "life is essentially a cheat . . . and that the redeeming things are not 'happiness and pleasure' but the deeper satisfactions that come out of struggle," he always remained someone who depended to an unhealthy extent on the good opinion of others. And it was this dichotomy—the receptiveness to life's most profound lessons coupled with a need to win over the world by the force of his personality—that made him capable of being, in equal measure, aesthetically rigid and conspicuously manipulative.

In the end, Fitzgerald's attitude toward Hollywood was as inconsistent as his attitudes toward everything. The warring impulses in him never really subsided. He was alternately sensible and reckless; worldly and adolescent; down to earth and somewhere above Alpha Centauri. He said that he knew more about life in his books than he did in life, and he was right. In life, he simply wanted too much. He wanted to be both a great novelist and a Hollywood hot shot. He wanted to box like Gene Tunney and run downfield like Red Grange. He wanted to write songs like Cole Porter and poetry like John Keats. He wanted the trappings of wealth, but was drawn to the social idealism of Marx. He wasn't so much a walking contradiction as a quivering mass of dreams and ambitions that, depending on how he was feeling and whom he was talking to, created a dizzying array of impressions. Anita Loos noticed that people in Hollywood "treated him like an invalid," and George Cukor found him "very grim, dim, slightly plump." Anthony Powell, however, after having lunch with Fitzgerald in the MGM commissary, noticed "a schoolmasterish streak, if at the same time an attractive one; an enthusiasm, simplicity of exposition, that might have offered a career as a teacher or university don." Fitzgerald's own schoolmaster at Princeton, Christian Gauss, would not have been surprised by these disparate opinions. Fitzgerald, he said, reminded him of all the Karamazov brothers at once.

In Hollywood, the brothers were continually elbowing each other aside. One day, screenwriting could be a "tense crossword puzzle game . . . a surprisingly interesting intellectual exercise"; the next day, it might represent "a rankling indignity." Unresolved feelings bubbled up in him to the very end: "Isn't Hollywood a dump," he wrote to a friend in 1940, "in the human sense of the word. A hideous town, pointed up by the insulting gardens of its rich, full of the human spirit at a new low of debasement." Sure it was— but it was also, as he well knew, part of the American character. It was Hollywood that lay stretched out before him when he jotted in his notes for *The Love of the Last Tycoon*, "I look out at it—and I think it is the most beautiful history in the world. It is the history of me and of my people . . . It is the history of all aspiration—not just the American dream but the human dream and if I came at the end of it that too is a place in the line of the pioneers."

Such words remind us that Fitzgerald drew his faith not from camera angles or even plotlines but from sentences; and what draws us powerfully to his work is the sensitive handling of emotional yearning and regret. When he was revising *Gatsby*, he characterized the burden of the novel as "the loss of those illusions that give such color to the world so that you don't care whether things are true or false as long as they partake of the magical glory." As Arthur Mizener, Fitzgerald's first biographer, pointed out, "It is precisely this loss which allows Gatsby to discover what a grotesque thing a rose is and how raw the sunlight was upon the scarcely created grass." Perhaps Fitzgerald could have captured this heightened state of awareness in a script, but was this what the studios were looking for? Fitzgerald's vision of becoming a great screen-writer was no more realistic than the likelihood of his returning a kickoff or writing a hit Broadway show. But, then, Fitzgerald was not one to give up on dreams; if he had, he could not have written so beautifully, so penetratingly, about their loss.

10

THE WORST OF TIMES

Revisiting the Great Depression

A funny thing happened on the way to eternity: the longer
that history stretched, the shorter the intervals that historians
studied. In fact, it wasn't long ago that historians thought
exclusively in large swaths of time, addressing the ages and
epochs that enfolded a hundred-years war, the fall of an
empire, or a renaissance in art and literature. But as time
marched on and documentation accumulated, scholars began
to fasten on the years and seasons that captured a trend. Possibly the first history to register a full retreat from the increasingly large heap of facts was Thomas Beer's *The Mauve Decade*
(1926), which confined itself to a survey of the 1890s. Since
then we have welcomed, among others, Alethea Hayter's *A
Sultry Month: Scenes of London Literary Life in 1846,* centering on
the suicide of the painter Benjamin Robert Haydon, and Pene-
lope Hughes-Hallet's *The Immortal Dinner: A Famous Evening of
Genius and Laughter in Literary London, 1817,* which again takes
up the story of Haydon and his circle. Decades, in particular,
seem to fascinate us and few pass by without someone letting
us know what they meant.

The tendency to cordon off history is understandable, but can the essence of a decade truly be bracketed by numbers? Well, no. Discrete events have their beginnings and endings, but their implications may linger for a long and indeterminate time. That said, there are certain decades that do possess— both by complexion and positioning—fairly well-defined boundaries: the nineteen-thirties, for example, stamped at one end by the stock market crash of 1929 and at the other by America's entry, in 1941, into the Second World War. The years in between, of course, have become known as The Great Depression[1]—a period when 34 million Americans (out of a population of 123 million) had no means of earning a living, when roughly 2 million homeless made up a "wandering population," and 15 million—25 percent of the workforce—were idle. By 1932 the economy had deteriorated to such an extent that men set forest fires so that they could be hired to put them out and committed crimes because jails, at least, served food. For the first time in the country's history, the number of people leaving America was greater than the number of those arriving. Asked whether there had ever been such an economic downturn, John Maynard Keynes replied, "Yes. It was called the Dark Ages, and it lasted four hundred years."

Nonetheless, the country did not shut down; in fact, a small number of businesses actually managed to thrive. Refrigerators and radios sold briskly; so did cigarettes and contraceptives. People bowled, played miniature golf, and went to ball games and the movies. Tourism increased, and motels

---

[1] "Depression" was not the loaded word it is now. The Hoover administration adopted the term because it sounded less inflammatory than "crisis" or "panic." It was only in 1931 that Hoover began to refer to "a great depression," careful to use the indefinite article. "The Great Depression," as shorthand for the 1930s, may not have appeared until the British economist Lionel Robbins used it as a book title in 1934.

sprang up nationwide. And because wages in some cases stayed ahead of the cost of living, those who found decent jobs or who held on to them actually fared better than they had before the crash. Most Americans, it bears remembering, were employed during the Depression, and a few, like Edmund Wilson, regarded the decline as cause for celebration: "To the writers and artists of my generation who had grown up in the Big Business era," Wilson wrote, "these years were not depressing but stimulating. One couldn't help being exhilarated at the sudden unexpected collapse of that stupid gigantic fraud. It gave us a new sense of freedom; and it gave us a new sense of power to find ourselves carrying on while the bankers, for a change, were taking a beating." Spoken like a true intellectual, more concerned with the fall of the mighty than with the welfare of those who depend on a stable economy.

The majority of Americans obviously felt otherwise, yet Wilson's blithe pronouncement does suggest that "the Thirties," despite having an evocative, instantly recognizable tag, was not some monolithic period in American history. Indeed, as Morris Dickstein vigorously reminds us in *Dancing in the Dark*, it was also the decade of screwball comedies, backstage musicals, gangster movies, jazz, art deco friezes, and theatrical concoctions featuring effervescent tunes and highly elaborate dance numbers. "Trying to grasp the essential spirit of the thirties would seem to be a hopeless task," Dickstein acknowledges. "How can one era have produced both Woody Guthrie and Rudy Vallee, both the Rockettes high-stepping at the Radio City Music Hall and the Okies on their desperate trek toward the pastures of plenty in California?" And because culture is not homogenous, because there is always an undercurrent flowing counter to what appears on the surface, it behooves us to remember that no period is without a healthy dose of self-contradiction.

At the very heart of the Depression was a paradox that, in retrospect, both questioned and affirmed the state of the union. As the nation's fortunes tumbled and men and women lost their jobs and homes, it was only natural that many felt a sense of betrayal. If jobs did not exist for those willing to work, if business leaders did not know what they were doing, if America was not necessarily the land of opportunity, then what was the country about? At the very moment when the phrase "the American dream" gained currency with the publication of James Truslow Adams's *The Epic of America* in 1931, Americans began to ask themselves whether the dream was nothing more than a cruel joke.

Since the nation's founding, people believed or pretended to believe that America was fundamentally a classless society, or one in which class borders were porous enough to accommodate the Horatio Alger myth of the poor boy who makes good. "There is no permanent class of hired laborers amongst us," Abraham Lincoln noted a year before he was elected president. "Twenty-five years ago I was a hired laborer. The hired laborer of yesterday labors on his own account today, and will hire others to labor for him tomorrow." It didn't matter that only a precious few ever rose above their circumstances; social mobility was the bedrock of the American dream. As long as there was *one* Abraham Lincoln, *one* Andrew Carnegie, one Jack Dempsey, *one* poor boy who lifted himself up by his bootstraps, then every white male, at any rate, could make it. But if there were no jobs to be had, how was a person to survive, much less rise? That was the question the Great Depression posed.

Yet even as the Depression was playing havoc with men's lives, it stirred a populist feeling that resisted attempts to alter the very political system that was responsible for the general misery. It was as if the Depression, by denying men the means of providing for their families, also confirmed the American ethos of individualism and self-reliance. For Communists and other radicals, however, the Depression was a gift, proof that capitalism was a sham. Hoping to take advantage of the economic slide, the Party, under orders from Moscow, renounced its agenda of class warfare and encouraged a "Popular Front" that aligned itself with liberals, socialists, and unionists—the better to fight fascism. Although this newer, gentler communism, appealed to many New Dealers, it never succeeded in gaining a true foothold. Most poor and middle-class Americans, however badly they were faring, kept faith with the country that was now disappointing them.

Historians agree that the Depression emerged at a moment when innovative developments in technology enabled artists, writers, filmmakers, photographers, and musicians, as well as politicians and social reformers, to portray the economic crisis in ways of their own devising. Such public displays and forums not only shaped a new picture of the nation but also bestowed on its citizens a greater sense of community. Affordable cameras, radios, and phonographs helped promote a more intimate sense of America, as did the newsreel with its sappy, patriotic voice-over. Hollywood, of course, came out swinging, often literally, by producing musicals that were meant to make people forget their troubles. Movies, however, still had to compete with radio for an audience; one program, *Amos 'n' Andy*, was so popular that theaters scheduled their show times around it.

Whether the Depression was spoken of or left unmentioned didn't matter; it was the subtext of whatever played on the air or ended up on the screen.[2] For Dickstein this constituted still another cultural dichotomy, namely, the simultaneous grappling with social issues and the desire to escape from them through entertainment. This struggle between living in the Depression and thinking outside it was also reflected by artists, whose sense of social responsibility was, to some degree, at odds with a "technically innovative modernism" that focused more on conveying complex states of consciousness than on the ills of society. So much poverty and misery in the land could not be ignored by artists who, after all, were sometimes strapped for cash themselves. John Steinbeck, for one, could not afford postage in 1932, much less a dentist for his rotting teeth.

The Depression was not the first time that writers and artists had looked at the underclass (Zola's *Germinal*, van Gogh's *Potato Eaters*, and Jacob Riis's halftone images in *How the Other Half Lives* acknowledged the wretched conditions of the poor), but the Depression did, as Dickstein notes, make artists identify "strongly with ordinary people and their needs." By and large, there had been little organized sympathy for the poor. Most Americans felt comfortable with a brand of social Darwinism in which economic individualism and moral rectitude were linked. If people were poor, they had only themselves to blame. But once a great many *more* people lost

[2] The first owners of radio stations publicized only their own wares; it never occurred to them to sell "time" to unrelated businesses, just as they didn't think to transmit music that was not live. Playing records on the air did not catch on until a New York reporter resorted to them during breaks in the Lindbergh Baby kidnapping trial in 1935. While playing records, the reporter pretended to be in a ballroom listening to a real band. For his efforts, he was disapprovingly dubbed a disc jockey by the columnist Walter Winchell, but his broadcasting ruse became *The Make-Believe Ballroom* and lasted on the air until the late Eighties.

their jobs, and certain writers (Michael Gold and Henry Roth) recorded the misery they grew up with, while others (Steinbeck and Nelson Algren) registered the misery they came to know, the poor began to be regarded more humanely. Suddenly, they were everywhere: tenant farmers, tenement dwellers, migrant families, and filthy hobos—all described in exacting detail or discovered peering out from photographs, newsreels, and movies.

A good number of these cultural efforts were underwritten by the federal government as part of the New Deal. The Works Progress Administration (WPA), for example, which lasted eight years, spent $11 billion and employed nearly 8 million men and women, including artists such as Jackson Pollock, Mark Rothko, and Willem de Kooning. Because the New Deal smacked of government meddling and welfare, it had its detractors. To justify its existence, one of the newly formed agencies, the Farm Security Administration, established a photography unit in order to document the harsh conditions of the poor. During its nine-year tenure, this unit, drawing on the talents of some of the nation's best photographers—including Margaret Bourke-White, Carl Mydans, and graphic artist Ben Shahn—created 77,000 black-and-white photographs, as well as the documentaries *The Plow That Broke the Plains* (1936) and *The River* (1937). The now iconic 1936 photo of a weathered migrant worker with her three children in Nipomo, California, was taken by Farm Security Administration photographer Dorothea Lange.

Apparently, a depression of unprecedented misery was necessary before writers and artists felt moved to humanize the poor and before the arts and the government could enter into a partnership. Whether it was because the WPA commissioned them or because of their own sympathy with the huddled masses, artists and journalists scoured the country to bring us news of how its citizens were coping. And the news came in the form of novels and poems, posters and paintings, speeches and plays, songs and films. Dickstein welcomes them all, displaying an unnervingly comprehensive grasp of every genre. As a result, *Dancing in the Dark* is, to risk over-statement, a monumental work, both a prodigious feat of labor and, in some instances, a labor of love. So wide is its net that it's practically impossible to convey the expanse of materials or the steadiness with which Dickstein handles them. It's not just Steinbeck and Odets who come in for analysis but Woody Guthrie and Cole Porter; not just Richard Wright and Zora Neale Hurston but Bing Crosby and Cary Grant; not just F. Scott Fitzgerald and Aaron Copland but James Agee and Louis Armstrong. And because the Thirties were "a turning point in American popular culture," Dickstein, poor chap, had no choice but to immerse himself in all the great movies and songs that exploded on the scene.

Unlike academics of the Seventies and Eighties, Dickstein does not exact semiotic significance from popular entertainment. Nor does he lend credence to the New Historicist dictum, fashionable twenty years ago, that "Mickey Mouse may in fact be more important to an understanding of the 1930s than Franklin Roosevelt." (The mouse barely rates a mention in Dickstein's book.) But Dickstein does believe—and rightly so—that "somehow movies became a significant part of how the American people adapted to the Depression." As it happened, the consolidation of the movie studios coincided with the onset of the Depression, and Hollywood writers and directors applied themselves to depicting the American scene, churning out an astonishing number of movies, of which an astonishing number were very good. At the same time, Hollywood wanted to offer relief from the Depression and looked for scripts of a fantastic or quietly fabulist kind. Dickstein concedes that "no easy contrast can be drawn between escapism and social relevance," but he happily wades in, trying to relate movies to the mood of the country.

In most instances, he does this with panache, though every so often he'll resort to a bland generalization so sweeping as to be puncture-proof: "Movie audiences dreamed of success, of magical changes of fortune, yet also identified with failure, which seemed closer to the reality of people's lives." To his credit, he also picks up on numerous subtleties that enhance our appreciation. Gangster films, for example, are both immigrant fables and parodies of Horatio Alger success stories whose you-can't-push-me-around attitude appealed to men who were being pushed out of jobs and homes. And if the gangster was not a good guy, it was society that made him that way; likewise with such Thirties films as *King Kong*, *Frankenstein*, and *The Invisible Man*, whose flawed protagonists lashed out only when hurt (not like the alien and malignant creatures who arrived on the screen in the Fifties and Sixties).

As both a critic and a fan, Dickstein has every right to expatiate on films and, for that matter, on Broadway shows and the lyrics and melodies of pop tunes. He's engaging and astute about Frank Capra's movies and the music of Cole Porter and George and Ira Gershwin. He's probably watched every Fred Astaire movie ever made and neatly sums up what can't be proved but needs saying anyway: "The culture of elegance, as represented by Astaire and the Gershwins, was less about the cut of your tie and tails than about the cut of your feelings, the inner radiance that was one true bastion against social suffering." But does he occasionally swoon too much? Although there may be sublimated currents of sexual energy in Ginger Rogers and Fred Astaire movies, Dickstein's contention that had such energy "been harnessed to some larger social purpose, as the New Deal had hoped to do, it might have brought the Depression to a swift end" is the sort of portentous remark that an editor should have excised. Dickstein obviously loves Fred and Ginger, but I'm not sure that the plot lines of their films require explication or that the choreography improves upon our hearing that it constitutes a mobility denied the people during the 1930s. And when Dickstein expounds on the rococo productions of Busby Berkeley, whose "skill at orchestrating grouped masses in precise formulations belonged to the collective side of the 1930s outlook," one might be forgiven a quiet "Oh, please." Yes, Busby Berkeley is more germane to the Depression than Bishop Berkeley, but who thinks of bread lines when the camera pans back and fifty pairs of sequined legs kick up in the air?

Culture and the arts have always had an uneasy relationship: one derives its essential quality from the general; the other, from the particular. A cultural history, therefore, must resist a natural tendency to squeeze both culture and art into a social-psychological box, a tendency that grows stronger the more extreme the times become. Because the Depression landed artists in the same foxhole as ordinary people, and because there are probably even fewer aesthetes in foxholes than atheists, many creative types felt it was unseemly to pursue purely aesthetic goals against a backdrop of human suffering. So writers such as Dos Passos and composers such as Copland had to balance progressive ideals with the aesthetic refinements of modernism. On the other hand, Faulkner, Wallace Stevens, Hemingway, and Fitzgerald would have written pretty much the same whatever the GNP. That's the tension in Dickstein's own book: he believes in the singularity of art, yet strives mightily to relate everything to the Depression.

Accordingly, there is both veneration for individual works and a New Historicist's capacious, almost anthropological approach to events, in which nothing falls outside of culture, and differences themselves inevitably, if obliquely, suggest a common source or reference point: "The look of the great thirties musicals," Dickstein writes, "is everything that Dorothea Lange's 'Migrant Mother' or 'Woman of the High Plains,' both so angular and static, are not. It's all circle and swirl, all movement and flow." Fine, but what does this tell us except that culture can be varied or paradoxical?

The truth is that art is not simply a socialized phenomenon, not one text among a myriad of texts, but a unique contribution to an ongoing discussion with other artists past and present. No doubt the French Revolution influenced Wordsworth and Coleridge, no doubt at all that Napoleon inspired Beethoven, but motivation is not to be confused with meaning: the French Revolution does not explain the *Lyrical Ballads*; Napoleon does not explain the *Eroica*. The Depression was responsible for many kinds of art, but it ultimately cannot account for whatever quality defines something as art. Dickstein recognizes this and settles on an inoffensive parallelism to describe the relation between art and history. Indeed, some form of the word "parallel" appears time and again in the book, as in "the expressive culture of the thirties . . . played a role parallel to the leadership of FDR and the programs of the New Deal," and "the uncompromising aesthetic radicalism of Copland or Dos Passos paralleled the political radicalism of the Left during the early thirties."

Stylistic tics aside, *Dancing in the Dark* offers a clue to the making of modern America, an America whose awareness of itself as a communal entity took shape during the Depression. It's a tricky proposition, trying to determine when a people form a sense of themselves as a national entity, or to what extent this entity represents their beliefs and ideals. Borders are the least of it; something more intangible is involved: a common language and heritage, which, as we know, keep evolving. The past is always being manipulated, and the recoverable past—what sticks in the minds of the populace at any one time—is often a collection of myths, popular conceptions, and fanciful images. But it is precisely these things—the stories that are repeated, the images that are represented, the music and lyrics that play in our heads—that contribute to a sense of a nation's character; not its constitution, or its charter, or its laws.

It can be argued that the consumer culture of the 1920s, along with the ascendancy of sports, entertainment, and advertising, was already blunting America's ingrained sectionalism. One could just as easily make the case that the Great Depression, which put so many people in the same predicament, significantly enhanced a sense of unity. The Depression, after all, summoned Franklin Roosevelt, who initiated the New Deal, which made use of the arts to call attention to the collective plight of the people, thus fostering a wave of populism that began in Washington, D.C. and spread to Hollywood, California, where it was spun around and sent back to the capital in the form of sentimental movies extolling "the people." Hollywood executives had no love for radicals and did not see an America that was inherently flawed but one in which the common man was the exemplary man. Whether his name was John Doe, Jefferson Smith, George Bailey, or Longfellow Deeds, he embodied the populist as well as the individual qualities that made this country unique. *In Meet*

John Doe (1941), Gary Cooper, the quintessential American hero, says to a gathering of unemployed men:

> I know a lot of you are saying, What can I do, I'm just a little punk. I don't count. Well, you're dead wrong. The little punks have always counted, because in the long run the character of a country is the sum total of its little punks. But we've all got to get in there and pitch.

Apart from the Civil War, the Great Depression probably affected the lives of more Americans than any one phenomenon in the nation's history, but it did not become a national trauma until the media made it one. In effect, it wasn't the Depression that helped unify the country but information about it: the books and movies, the photographs and newsreels, the radio programs, especially FDR's fireside chats, that made Americans feel part of a common culture. How much of this culture remains is anyone's guess. Now, with cable TV and satellite radio and online echo chambers that customize experiences rather than consolidate them, the prospect that the current financial mess will elicit the kind of grand communal response Dickstein describes seems remote. Indeed, we may have reached a point at which digital clutter succeeds only in accentuating differences rather than overriding them. Once upon a time, a few powerful radio stations, a few large newspapers, and a few network TV channels caught or created a *national* mood. But that world, for good or for ill, has been supplanted by a predominantly virtual world to which every person can contribute, thus making the idea of a unified national culture more problematic than ever. Dickstein may not have steered his book toward such questions, but it is a measure of the work's timeliness and historical grasp that we arrive at these questions nonetheless.

11

THE LONG GOODBYE

The Sixties—*In Pace Requiem*

An African American is president of the United States. I am too old to write this without shaking my head in amazement. If a woman were president today, I might also feel surprise, but not because the nation had suddenly swerved off its intended course. Whatever inequities women in America have endured over the centuries, the sight of a black man taking the oath of office simply had too much history attached to it. Standing behind Obama were slaves working in the fields, sold at auction, or hanging from a rope. Standing closer were those still alive, participants in the civil rights struggles of the 1960s, for whom segregation had been a fact of life. For these middle-aged and elderly black people, it was as if history had finally absolved the decade of its mistakes and excesses. As for the rest of us, especially those who "lived the Sixties," it seemed as if the decade was finally being laid to rest.

The mild irony here is that the Sixties had to be resurrected before they could be retired. Each time that Hilary Clinton and Barack Obama faced each other as candidates for the Democratic nomination, a faint echo of the Sixties pealed forth. It was in the Sixties, after all, when the process began that allowed a woman and an African American, nearly fifty years later, a chance at the presidency. Hence, the weirdly discordant feeling of watching Clinton and Obama clash for the nomination while simultaneously witnessing the exploitation of Obama's pastor in order to discredit his candidacy.

Although the stage-hugging Jeremiah Wright seems to have left the public arena, the surfacing of his 2005 "God Damn America" sermon served a useful purpose. The video summoned from Obama his seminal speech on race as well as the acknowledgment that Wright, who was born in 1941, was still "fighting the fights of the Sixties," as if this somehow exonerated him—and, to an extent, it did. Political persuasions aside, there is no denying the institutional racism that existed—especially in the South—until the 1960s. Had cable channels, which were so fond of repeatedly looping snippets of Wright's sermon, spliced his exhortations with shots of the segregated buses, water fountains, restaurants, and schools that dominated the American landscape fifty years ago, more viewers might have understood what lay behind the inflammatory language. From Wright on the pulpit in Chicago in 2003, we could have cut to Governor George Wallace at his inauguration in 1963, declaiming, "Segregation today, segregation tomorrow, segregation forever." Now fade to footage of the dogs, billy clubs, cattle prods, and fire hoses that were used on nonviolent demonstrators in Selma and Birmingham around that time. Blacks who came of age in the Sixties are still angry? What a shock.

Historians agree that the long legislative battle for civil rights came to a head in the Sixties, culminating in the Civil Rights Act of 1964 and the Voting Rights Act of 1965. Unfortunately, there is little else about the Sixties that historians agree on, including when the era (as an ethos) began, when it ended, and what it ultimately meant. But they do concur that it was a most unusual and unusually significant decade in the nation's evolution. Now, however, comes *The Sixties Unplugged* by Gerard J. DeGroot, which rather defiantly interprets the decade's prominence as more fabrication than fact, whose most salient feature was its lack of "coherent logic."

Disorder cannot shape historical narrative, so DeGroot has hit on a kaleidoscopic approach to convey the helter-skelter of those years, and the resulting narrative, though not a jumble, owes little to consecutiveness. As such, *The Sixties Unplugged* is history with a difference or, at least, history without borders. Not proffered as an exhaustive study of the decade, it is, DeGroot contends, "more global than any book previously produced." He may be right. The book's sixty-seven autonomous sections—dealing with everything from sit-ins in Albany, Georgia, to riots in Sharpeville, South Africa; from the Cultural Revolution in China to the Six-Day War in Israel; and from a U.S.-assisted coup in Jakarta to the chaotic revolt of Parisian students in 1968—serve to remind us that the Sixties were not confined to America but were an international phenomenon.

Nonetheless, it's America that DeGroot returns to time and again, for the oft-stated reason that we continue to saddle the decade with more significance than it can possibly bear. According to DeGroot, the Sixties hang in our collective living room like the head of some wondrous beast, eliciting reflexively both disgust and admiration. Either the decade was a hallowed time that produced something of lasting social worth, or it was an aberrant period whose cultural legacy is the skewering of American values and traditions. DeGroot thinks we should get past this. Take a good look at the decade, he admonishes: conflict, dissension, and bloodshed are not unique to one time; the Sixties in America and elsewhere was just another ten-year interval in a bloody series of such intervals. If you look closely and then step back and take in the long view, the decade was neither "unfamiliar nor all that special."

I don't think so. Although a contrarian strain and a distrust of government have been present in America since the days of the Whiskey Rebellion, the bitterness and carnage of the late Sixties stand apart. According to the findings of the Senate Subcommittee on Government Operations, over one hundred cities from 1965 through 1968 experienced riots: 189 people were killed, 7,614 injured, and 59,257 arrested. After the invasion of Cambodia in 1970 and the killing of four unarmed students at Kent State University in May (two more were killed later that month at Jackson State College in Mississippi), a national student strike shut down some five hundred campuses, and half of the nation's students are said to have participated in one kind of protest or another.(DeGroot himself acknowledges that more than 1,300 colleges and universities were affected and that 536 temporarily closed their doors.) To some it seemed as if the country was more divided at that moment than at any time since the Civil War.

In truth, the Sixties were an assault on the senses. Nothing may have equaled the horror, sensory overload, and almost surrealistic violations of September 11, 2001, but the late Sixties consisted of one gut-wrenching event after another; one crescendo barely dying down before another began to build. In 1967 the civil rights movement birthed a violent Black Power offspring. ("Stop singing and start swinging. Get a gun," H. Rap Brown, head of the Student Nonviolent Coordinating Committee, ordered his followers.) In January of 1968, the Tet Offensive disabused us of the belief that the United

States was going to end the war in Vietnam quickly. In March, Lyndon Johnson announced that he would not seek reelection; in April, Martin Luther King Jr. was assassinated; two months later, so was Robert Kennedy. That spring, Columbia students occupied the offices of the university's president and had to be forcibly removed by the police. In August, the Democratic National Convention deteriorated into a brutal melee between police and demonstrators.[1]

Not "all that special"?

Things got worse before they got better, and the ensuing years, in the words of Morris Dickstein, constituted "the unfinished business of the Sixties": the campus shootings, the fall of Saigon, the end of the compulsory draft, the release of the Pentagon Papers, Watergate, Nixon's resignation. Before long, even straight students and middle-of-the-road Americans began to feel revulsion toward a government that napalmed civilians in Asia and gunned down civilians in Ohio.

DeGroot doesn't lower the flame; he just confines the heat to urban ghettos and college campuses. He knows the Sixties were divisive; otherwise those who write about them wouldn't surrender to the biases that "give rise to a misleading, reductive image." DeGroot, who was born in 1955, assures us that he formed *his* "opinions on the basis of recent research rather than on golden memories of a life once lived." This specified unlived life enables him to write:

> After the decade died, it arose again as a religion. For quite
> a few people, the Sixties is neither memory nor myth, but

---

[1] Almost lost in the maelstrom of 1968 was the death of Neal Cassady, hero to the Beats, driver of the Merry Prankster bus, and inspiration for various characters in Kerouac's *Road* novels. What better sign that the Fifties brand of rebellion had come to an end?

faith . . . The believers worship a few martyred gods (Che, Lennon, Kennedy, King, Lumumba) and seek truth in the teachings of an assortment of sometimes competing prophets (Malcolm X, Leary, Hoffman, Hendrix, Dylan, Dutschke, Muhammad Ali, et al.)

This, I'm not reluctant to say, is a straw man of almost gargantuan proportions. What is this creed DeGroot thinks we have created and continue to hold dear? With whom do these golden memories reside? Outside of a few tenured radicals and doe-eyed communards, does anyone believe that "bliss was it in that dawn to be alive"? Todd Gitlin, an early member of Students for a Democratic Society (SDS) and still a man of the Left, noted eleven years ago that "only a few desperate, unreconciled souls today embrace what is called 'the sixties' wholeheartedly." To be sure, Bob Dylan has his worshipful commentators—the critic Christopher Ricks and the historian Sean Wilentz being the most cogent—but no one I ever met, who hadn't bonged his way into a hospital ward, followed the "teachings" of Leary, Hendrix, or Ali. (What exactly were Jimi's teachings?) As for John and Robert Kennedy—enough revisionist histories of Camelot have been published during the past twenty years to make even their staunchest admirers blanch.

DeGroot is rather keen on the fact that student activists made up only a small fraction of the student population, and that Americans in general, even if they disapproved of the war in Vietnam, were opposed to disruptive or militant tactics. He doesn't want us to forget that "The Ballad of the Green Berets" outsold "Give Peace a Chance." Quite so. Only a handful of students around the country were true believers, and only a small percentage felt, as Gitlin did, that being young in America during the Sixties meant feeling "betrayed" and "enraged." The majority of students who marched against the war in Vietnam had no carefully thought-out political philosophy. They marched because they were reacting to images of police brutality and the tragic actions of a few criminally stupid National Guardsmen. Just because you smoked dope and thought Nixon was a creep didn't mean that you spent hours discussing Frantz Fanon's *Wretched of the Earth*.

I'm willing to go even further than DeGroot. The counter-culture and the uniform it adopted—the long hair and loose clothes—concealed con men, charlatans, pushers, and the occasional psychopath. Although a core of idealistic young men and women briefly thought they could influence foreign policy and improve the lot of poor people and minorities, they soon splintered into various interest groups and by the early 1970s were gone from the scene. And despite the manifest presence of socially conscious activists and serious-minded community organizers, I can't help wondering how many students became part of the Sixties because they were drifting with the times or just wanted to take advantage of them. At long last, a kid in school didn't have to be a jock or cool in the Fonzie mode to meet girls. If you were sensitive and fiercely anti-establishment, if you could quote Blake or Che, chances were good you might meet someone who liked you for your politics. In other words, nerds and geeks by join-ing the counterculture could get laid. But so what? If the Six-ties were not an authentically utopian movement, if they did not consist purely of selfless acts based on moral idealism, that doesn't mean they were without redeeming value.

But such value, DeGroot insists, is more imagined than real. Echoing William McGill, the former chancellor of the University of California at San Diego, DeGroot mocks "the nostalgia merchants who have turned the sixties into a decade of glorious achievement." This, too, beggars belief. More historians and writers have trained a gimlet eye on the Sixties than on any other decade in this nation's history except possibly the one that occurred a hundred years earlier. Scholars may evince a bias without necessarily distorting the historical record, and readers are free to add or subtract emphasis. If Tom Hayden seems at times nostalgic, and Allan Bloom frequently dyspeptic, readers can decide for themselves whose bias bears better witness.

For a determinedly disinterested observer, DeGroot can sound suspiciously like Vice President Spiro Agnew (a Sixties bugbear, whose plea of *nolo contendere* to charges of tax evasion and bribery in 1973 gave pleasure to millions), but that doesn't mean he's always wrong. Student protesters may not have been "an effete crop of impudent snobs who consider themselves intellectual," as Agnew famously said (and William Safire less famously wrote), but the movement *was* fueled in part by what DeGroot describes as "the high-octane naiveté of self-important young people who have just discovered 'eternal truths.'" What's irritating about DeGroot's accusations is not their substance but their claim to uniqueness.

DeGroot is not the first to point out that the antiwar movement was a failure and that student protests had little or no effect on the government's handling of the war. But this is a far cry from pronouncing that the Sixties were "an era of magnificent futility." The antiwar movement was part of a larger cultural shift whose influence persists to this day. Despite having won the White House five times since 1980, conservatives have never stopped bristling at the thought of the Sixties. "To me all the problems began in the Sixties," former House Majority Leader Dick Armey told *The New Republic* in 1995. He was alluding to the usual problems that conservatives believe are propagated by the schools, foundations, art coun-cils and, of course, the liberal media: identity politics, political correctness, the collapse of the nuclear family, a perversion of sexual mores, a decline in civility, and a disregard for the law.

However one feels about this cultural "liberalization," the least we can do is admit that it came about precisely because of establishment politics. The war in Vietnam, the activities of the CIA in Africa and Asia, and the treatment of minorities and women created the tenured radicals who would exact a kind of vengeance on the high culture that the establishment took for granted. From the early 1970s to the mid-1990s, left-ist intellectuals and bookish conservatives battled over the humanities, each side operating on the assumption that poli-tics and aesthetics could not be separated. So liberal critics like Morris Dickstein *had* to like Allen Ginsberg, and conserv-ative critics like Roger Kimball had to dislike him.[2]

But let's take a moment. Contrary to the presumptive boundaries of the culture wars, one didn't have to vote the Republican ticket to disapprove of academic claptrap and the jettisoning of standards. You could be young and liberal and still feel that many of Norman Mailer's posturings—not only his desire for the apocalyptic orgasm—were just plain hooey. In fact, you could smoke dope and read Jane Austen, drop acid and attend a performance of *Don Giovanni*, take part in a demonstration, return home, wash the tear gas out of your eyes, put on a recording of Bach's "Musical Offering," and fall asleep with Keats's sonnets in your hands.

---

[2] Anyone interested in the artistic and intellectual currents of the Sixties can do no better than to consult Roger Kimball's wonderfully draconian *The Long March* and Morris Dickstein's more measured *Gates of Eden*. Dickstein's introduction to the 1997 edition offers an excellent summary of the Sixties' aftermath.

Although DeGroot confines himself to the period between 1960 and 1970, the Sixties both began and ended later. The first few years were simply the Fifties with a fresher, more energetic feel to them. The election of John F. Kennedy, young, vigorous, and hatless at his inauguration in 1961, elated many young Democrats, but it was still politics as usual, the same backroom politics that gained him the nomination in the first place. People went about their business, cut and combed their hair, drank whiskey sours or martinis at lunch, and dreaded the prospect of nuclear war. In 1964, schoolchildren practiced huddling under their desks in the event of an attack, just as they had in 1954.

I can only speak for an indeterminate number of white, middle-class males who attended college between 1965 and 1969 and who up to that point had not smoked a joint, kissed a breast, or encountered, as far as we knew, a homosexual of either sex. For us, the first year of college was pretty much what we had expected: classes, curfews, fraternities, mixers, football and basketball games, and bars, lots of bars. Although there were clear signs of growing unrest in black neighborhoods around the country, college campuses—aside from the occasional speechifying or mimeographed proclamation about the war or the CIA—were relatively quiet. No sense of solidarity distinguished campus life from life in the larger community. Then something happened. It wasn't the Gulf of Tonkin Resolution (a lot of us couldn't have found Vietnam on the map), nor was it racial tension or police actions (it wasn't until 1967 that the police were referred to, in an SDS memo, as "pigs"); it was something less tangible: a gradual awakening to the fact that students were a distinct subculture that, unlike bohemian enclaves in New York or San Francisco, was significant by virtue of numbers alone. By 1966, 40 percent of the U.S. population was under twenty-five, and with the number of troops in Vietnam having doubled in one year to nearly 400,000, students and non-students alike were becoming increasingly agitated by the draft.

Looking back, it seems to me it was between the winter of 1966 and the fall of 1967, between the release of "Revolver" and that of "Sgt. Pepper's Lonely Hearts Club Band," that the Sixties truly kicked in. No one remarked on it, but something in the air changed. One day we were going to football games and fraternity parties, the next we were getting stoned and wondering why we were taking pre-med courses. The Sixties happened, as Hemingway wrote in another context, "Gradually and then suddenly." Historians, however, require specificity. Some think they discern the first stirrings of the Sixties in the existential Fifties, in the alienated sensibility winding its way through Salinger's *Catcher in the Rye,* Camus's *The Stranger,* Sartre's *Nausea,* Ginsberg's *Howl,* and Brando's and James Dean's portrayals of sensitive yet manly loners. More literal-minded interpreters look to Kennedy's assassination in 1963 or the rise of the Free Speech Movement in '64. Still others equate the start of the decade to the Gulf of Tonkin Resolution in 1964, which enabled Johnson to increase the number of soldiers and bombing raids in Vietnam, thereby swelling the ranks of students opposed to the war.

In retrospect, the Sixties really began when it seemed as if there could be no turning back, when the war in Vietnam was amped up to such a degree that militants like Tom Hayden no longer had to go searching for recruits. It was Vietnam that drove the Sixties; without the anger the war occasioned, the drugs, the music, the communes, even the urban unrest might not have been sufficient to give the decade its distinctive and, yes, special coloring. In fact, had Johnson scaled back the fighting in 1966 or '67, he could have sought and won another term; Robert Kennedy would not have run for office and most likely would not have been assassinated; the draft would not have mobilized so many college students; and possibly a less violent strain of Black Power would have emerged from the civil rights movement. Indeed, had this scenario played out, as Todd Gitlin wistfully noted, then "despite growing global competition and Cold War Pressures, the country might have made a soft landing into a Newer Deal."

History is past and what's past is inevitable. One intriguing question remains: Why was this the first and only time that American college students rose up in large numbers to challenge the power structure? One of the more provocative books about the Sixties, Dominick Cavallo's *A Fiction of the Past*, makes a strong case that the youth culture of the Sixties acted on "the radical implications of the freedom, autonomy and democracy enshrined in their myths of national origins." Some of these myths, in transubstantiated form, were conveyed by electromagnetic waves in 1958, when five of the ten highest-rated weekly series happened to be Westerns. What did *Gunsmoke, Wagon Train, The Rifleman, The Virginian, Wyatt Earp, Maverick, Bonanza,* and *Have Gun, Will Travel* teach us? For one thing, they presented a West "dominated by violence and personal freedom, male aggressiveness and daring, geographical mobility and restlessness." They taught us to stand up for ourselves and against injustice (well, *Maverick* not so much). Yippie leader Jerry Rubin may have been kidding when he said that he had been "more influenced" by "the Lone Ranger . . . than by Mao or Che or Lenin," but he might also have been serious.

However we spin it—whether it was the alienation curdling in a materialistic consumer society or the failure of liberalism to steer the nation away from embroilment over-seas—the Sixties in the end were about the adults who made decisions based on a Cold War mentality and the children who were affected by those decisions. In the eyes of former National Security Adviser and Secretary of State Henry Kissinger, those children (the long-haired, unkempt protesters, at least) were acting on the lessons they had learned at home. Apparently the permissive child-rearing practices of the Fifties, as spelled out in the works of Dr. Benjamin Spock, fostered a generation of adolescents who felt themselves entitled to what they liked and exempt from what they didn't. Hence, the antiwar movement was driven, in Kissinger's words, by those who "had been brought up by skeptics, relativists, and psychiatrists; now they were rudderless in a world from which they demanded certainty without sacrifice." On the other hand, protesters may have been motivated by the senseless carnage of a war fought in a small country whose fall would not have toppled all the dominoes in the developing world. It could even be argued, as some have, that antiwar advocates had been raised to be "intensely competitive and individualistic" and were therefore more willing to reject traditions of "civic Republicanism and Puritanism's 'biblical' communitarianism."

The Sixties may not have begun with a wholesale resentment of the status quo, but the war and the separatist beliefs of Black Power activists ultimately created a rift between young and old, white and black, liberal (the Old Left) and radical (the New Left). By 1968 the rift had grown so deep that civil rights historian Taylor Branch wondered at the "almost overnight" disappearance of the American "ethos to hold out hope for and contact with one's enemies" The liberal tenet that rational action could improve the world suddenly

seemed toothless and naïve. Radicals didn't want to negotiate; they wanted out of the system. And the government
didn't conceal that it wanted them in jail or in the ground. The
enemy wasn't in Hanoi; it was in Hanover and in Houston.
And, given the absolute distrust that prevailed, one has to
wonder how many ethical or social positions were taken
because they differed from those of the establishment. To be
against the war in Vietnam was almost reflexive (a certain
amount of self-interest, after all, was involved), but was
it possible that we approved of homosexuality, in some
measure, because our fathers disapproved of it, and that we
engaged in indiscriminate sex because our mothers were
appalled by it?

We were not, of course, the first or last generation to regard
the world differently from our parents, but we were the first
to fetishize youth to an absurd degree, to confer on it a moral
dispensation. Innocence wasn't prized; insubordination was.
In the Fifties, boys and girls wanted to grow up, put on a
snappy fedora or mink stole, smoke cigarettes, mix drinks, get
married, and behave as adults. They may not have approved
of the way their parents ran things, but they also looked forward to the moment when *they* could run them. Sixties students however, didn't want to be in charge. I'm not speaking
of activists, or business majors, or members of Skull & Bones,
all of whom probably looked forward to entering the "real"
world, but of those who were content to shirk responsibility
until it was thrust upon them. Why rush into marriage, children, house, and job—"the full catastrophe," as Zorba the
Greek liked to say—when we could have fun?

The idea that adults had screwed things up meant that we
could and *should* behave differently from our parents. What
good was worldly ambition in a world that allowed the rise of

such callow operators as Henry Kissinger? Men of reason had bequeathed to us the Cold War, the military-industrial complex, the Bomb, the Vietnam War, and a society that, thus far, had taken the lives of 100 million people in the twentieth century. Why not rebel? Angry blacks took it to the streets; disenchanted whites took it to the hills. By 1970 there were some 4,000 communes dotting the American landscape.

It wasn't just the State that was to blame; it was also the state of things: the assumptions, rules of thought, and long-held values that had brought us to this pass. According to such Sixties thinkers as Herbert Marcuse *(Eros and Civilization)*, Norman O. Brown *(Life Against Death* and *Love's Body)*, Charles Reich *(The Greening of America)*, and R. D. Laing *(The Politics of Experience* and *The Divided Self)*, Western society was paying for the mistakes of the Enlightenment, which, broadly speaking, abjured the instinctive and the irrational. In the most general terms, and setting aside the very real differences between them, these books added up to a critique of reason. Western man was laboring under the illusion that the normal world was normal. By repressing out natural instincts we fell victim to a public neurosis that manifested itself in false social and sexual hierarchies and in the belief that sanity was synonymous with inhibition and conformity. Those who "got it" took off, as did Yossarian in *Catch 22* or the Chief in *One Flew Over the Cuckoo's Nest*. The problem wasn't the inmates but the officials who ran the asylums. That was the message in Philip de Broca's *King of Hearts* and Peter Weiss's *Marat/Sade*. If you wanted to see things as they really are, you had to drop out and/or drop acid, and find enlightenment in blends of Buddhism, Hinduism, astrology, Native Americanism, and Gnosticism.

The counterculture may not have succeeded in convincing most Americans that they lived in a particularly inequitable and racist society, but it did manage to make inroads in the national consciousness. Books and movies soon reflected new norms, different virtues, other expectations. The fiction of the 1960s and '70s, for example, made short work of the heroic attitude toward life (as embodied in the hardboiled persona) and gave us the insecure and immature man who, despite his age or intelligence, was never quite the adult his father had been. Even as Betty Friedan was calling for "a drastic reshaping of the cultural image of femininity," masculinity itself seemed to be getting a makeover. Robert Jordan shrank into Alex Portnoy; and instead of a new Gable, Cooper, Mitchum, or Bogart, we got Woody Allen, Dustin Hoffman, Richard Dreyfuss, and Jack Nicholson. And who should play Philip Marlowe, the quintessential private eye, in Robert Altman's *The Long Goodbye* but that quintessential antihero Elliott Gould. That just seemed wrong.

Culture is, clearly, far more complicated than individual novels and movies let on. The ordinary life rejected by the counterculture was precisely the life that most Americans wanted for themselves, and the vehemence of the protests only reaffirmed for them the values and stability found in marriage, religion, and hard work. Once the troops returned home and the riots and protests subsided, life became more or less normal again. It wasn't simply Watergate and Nixon's resignation that marked the end of the Sixties (those were outcomes of the Sixties); the Sixties were over when, in 1973 and '74, college students stripped naked and began streaking across campuses. What the hell was that about? It was about nothing and therefore unpardonably un-Sixties-like. And then, when Tony Manero, bell-bottomed and spangled, danced his way out of Brooklyn to the beat of the Bee Gees, you knew—you just knew—the Sixties were finished.

Except, that is, for the political and cultural residue they've left behind. As the 1960s wore on, working-class Americans began to associate the Democratic Party with student activism and black violence. Each time there was a violent takeover of a college or a shoot-out with the police, it played into the hands of the Republicans. And the nation—with an assist from the Democratic Party, which split, in 1968, into factions for Robert Kennedy, Gene McCarthy, and Hubert Humphrey—veered to the right. In 1968, Democratic nominee Hubert Humphrey received just 42.7 percent of the popular vote (four years later, George McGovern managed less than 40 percent, winning only the state of Massachusetts) as opposed to the 61.1 percent that Lyndon Johnson received in 1964.

Forty years after Nixon handily defeated the Democrats, a Democrat has carried the South, the Midwest, and those contested states that no Democrat was ever expected to win. Say what you want about the 1960s, they're the reason that Barack Obama is president. He didn't have to fight "the fights of the Sixties"; he is simply proof that the struggles paid off. It is a man of the Right, oddly enough, who struck the perfect note. After allowing that "our national life has been a running argument about, and with, the Sixties," George F. Will pointed out that whatever one thinks of it, "the decade is redeemed by what was done in bus terminals, at lunch counters, in voter registration drives on ramshackle porches along dangerous back roads and by all the other mining and sapping of the old system." To those who still harbor resentment: Give the Sixties their due and move on. The worst decade you know may be the one that's passing by now.

12

THE NIGHT MAN

Or Why I'm Not a Novelist

In 1972, when I was twenty-four years old, I took a job as a night watchman in a run-down hotel on Manhattan's Upper West Side. At the time, it seemed like the thing to do. In the 1970s, aspiring writers didn't become teachers or editors; they hired out as Alaskan guides, lumberjacks, or telephone linemen before attending the Iowa Writers' Workshop and hitting the creative-writing circuit. Well, I'd already put in time as a cab driver in New York and a *porteur* in the vineyards of Provence, and I didn't want to be a forest ranger or oyster diver, but night watchman had a certain déclassé appeal. Mind you, I was not a night clerk. Nathanael West had worked a night desk, which was fine for him, but I associated night clerks with sad, shady characters out of Raymond Chandler, one of those anonymous little men with a mustache "that gets stuck under your fingernail."

The place I had chosen to watch was Hayden Hall, a no-frills residential hotel between Amsterdam and Columbus Avenues. It was a small, sturdy building, seven stories high, with fourteen rooms and two communal bathrooms to a floor. With its colonnade of gray Ionic pillars beneath a sculpted pediment, and its Italianate frieze triangulating the windows, the hotel had an air of graceful formality. Once inside, however, you felt the sad, cramped life of the place. The lobby was no larger than a medium-sized living room, equipped with five unmatched chairs, a telephone booth, a cigarette machine, and a Formica counter that served as the front desk. The starkly lit hallways exposed peeling green walls and drab flower-print carpeting; and the rooms—the rooms were straight out of a noir film or Edward Hopper painting: a few rickety pieces of furniture, a sink and medicine cabinet, a linoleum-tiled floor, a window with a pull-down shade, and a bare overhead light bulb. My own room, small and yellow, overlooking an airshaft, was a space that a feng shui master would bite through glass to get out of.

The manager and part-owner of Hayden Hall was Isaac Sas, a narrow-shouldered, mournful-looking man of sixty, who paid me two dollars an hour while charging me twenty dollars a week for my room. Since almost a third of the ninety-eight rooms were usually unoccupied, I grumbled that I shouldn't have to pay rent. Why should I, when I wasn't replacing a paying customer? Sas, an old friend of my father's, whom I'd known nearly all my life, looked at me and scowled. "That's why I have to charge you; business is terrible."

My duties were simple. I worked the ancient boxy switchboard, the kind one saw in screwball comedies of the 1930s, with sets of plugged wires trailing from the console. After midnight I slid an iron bar between the handles of the heavy glass doors and leaned back and put my feet up. Three times during the night I put them down and rode the elevator to the seventh floor. From there I trooped down the stairs and inserted a triangular key into the round tape-clock situated on each floor that recorded, for insurance purposes, the time the floor was checked. I also made sure the communal bathrooms had an adequate supply of toilet paper.

I could handle it: I had an M.A. in English and Comparative Literature from Columbia. It wasn't a degree I had intended to get, but in the early Seventies a college graduate had three choices: continue with school, enter the military, or join the Peace Corps. I chose the first. But when a high lottery number freed me from both military duty and graduate school, I took off. It never occurred to me to look for full-time employment. I wanted, for lack of a better word, "experience." It sounds phony and in a way it was, since any articulated self-image is, by definition, manufactured. "Every man thinks meanly of himself for not having been a soldier, or not having been at sea," Dr. Johnson observed. But what if one is too conscious of this? What if one goes to war or to sea expressly to fulfill some ideal of manliness? Are you the real thing? Because I wanted to test myself, I lived and worked among men to whom such a test could never have occurred. I wasn't a roughneck in the Jack London mode who read Nietzsche; I was a guy who worked with roughnecks who didn't know London from Nietzsche.

And, of course, I wanted to be both the German philologist-philosopher and the American writer-adventurer. I had already written one unpublished novel and regularly submitted stories to *The New Yorker*, which were regularly declined with polite notes of encouragement. I figured it was only a matter of time. Until then I would work short-term jobs, evade responsibility, and write about my experiences. And because I was young—younger than I should have been at twenty-four—I thought that life—"real life"—took place outside of classrooms and offices. Real life was the lurid cover of a 1950's paperback novel: some guy with tousled hair and shirt sleeves rolled above the biceps, fending off a woman whose blouse was open to her navel. In short, Hayden Hall seemed the right place to be, a place where things might happen. So I made my rounds. I turned the key in the clocks. I dozed in the lobby. Occasionally, I dissuaded drunken tenants from bringing hookers back to their rooms. And when I went outside for a breath of air, I took along the iron bar. This was before comfy little bistros and elegant boutiques had come to Columbus Avenue, before one could safely walk the side streets between Amsterdam and Central Park West; in fact, the best thing you could say about Hayden Hall was that it was marginally better than the neighborhood.

Naturally, I figured on stumbling across characters out of Maupassant, Balzac, and Isherwood; I'd see and hear things that would make me another Chekhov or, at least, another John O'Hara. All I had to do was pay attention, be someone on whom nothing was lost, and the stories would write themselves. In *Down and Out in Paris and London*, George Orwell writes about a hotel in the Rue du Coq d'Or where the people were so poor that some had "fallen into solitary half-mad grooves of life and given up trying to be normal and decent." Unfortunately, the residents of Hayden Hall didn't answer to Orwell's description. For the most part, they were just ordinary, middle-aged, and elderly. The jobless men stayed in their rooms much of the time, going out only for meals, while the women, mostly heavy, with rouged cheeks and swollen feet, sat in the lobby making conversation that would put Harold Pinter to shame. I didn't know which was sadder: those who stopped by the desk to see if they had received calls or mail (but never did), or those who had given up asking. Late at night I would come across them on my rounds, scuttling to and from the common bathrooms, the women without makeup, the men without teeth; and we would pass each other in silence.

Not that the hotel didn't have its share of proper eccentrics. Among the old and the infirm was a group of five vaguely pretty women and two nondescript men—all in their twenties—who smoked dope, slept with each other, and treated everyone else with a disregard that bordered on mockery. They called themselves "Gnostics" and phoned each other frequently at all hours, even if they lived next door. After a while I ignored adjoining room numbers when they lit up on the switchboard. They complained to Sas, who told me sternly to connect them. "One moves out, they all move out," he said. I didn't care; I gambled with Sas's money. None of the other tenants were quite as obnoxious. There was, I recall, a tiny, dapper West Indian whose bonhomie verged on the pathological; an unwashed, long-haired racing tout who bragged of having slept with Joan Rivers as though he'd once hit a trifecta; and a spectral-thin, thirty-year-old laundry worker who wore a small cowbell around his neck. Every morning at 5:45, I would hear a faint tinkling from the staircase, and a moment later he'd step into the lobby. A few more jingles and he'd be out the door.

Aside from exchanging mean looks with the Gnostics, I had little to do with the hotel's residents. I worked at night and slept much of the day. And after a few weeks I became nocturnal, by which I mean something more than just staying up late. Lots of people stay up late—cops, firemen, nurses, interns, doormen, cab drivers—but they're not necessarily nocturnal; they're just working the late shift. Night people don't think about "late;" they think about where the action is: a party, a club, a card game, a place to score drugs or sex. And since I usually went to bed past midnight, it didn't take long for my body to adjust to its new schedule.

Becoming nocturnal meant, in effect, becoming someone else, someone who gradually drew away from friends and family, who became estranged from that part of society responsible for keeping society running. When you sleep much of the day and stay up all night, the world changes, and so do you. Different stimuli make for different perspectives. My habits changed, my meals changed, my thoughts changed, and for the few hours between mid-afternoon, when I awoke, and sunset, when I ate lunch, I felt exposed and out of step. Daytime stopped making sense. It was as if a new set of physical and ethical laws was taking shape. Not only did nightlife proceed at another pace, it accommodated behaviors that daylight could not entertain.

It wasn't just the after-hour clubs in the East Village where transvestites drank boilermakers till dawn or the strobe-lit Soho parties where porn films flickered on huge bare walls, it was also a lean man in a frayed black overcoat sitting on a stoop along Eighth Avenue. I'd spy him around three or four in the morning in the shadow of a darkened lamppost, an unlit cigarette dangling from his fingers. Even at that hour there were people out, and when someone passed too close, he'd call out in a whispery voice, "Got a light?" A few people stopped. Some fumbled for a book of matches, others whisked out a lighter. It was then he leaned forward, cigarette in hand—until his face came into the light, or what was left of it: one eyeless socket, a corrugated bump for a nose, and scar tissue like a smooth brown stocking pulled over his head. Whoever had bent solicitously toward him gasped and took a quick step back. Some women dropped their matchbooks, a few men managed to hold on to their lighters. But no one stayed a second longer then he or she had to. As for the man, he just chortled to himself and never bothered to pick up any of the matchbooks. For all I know, he didn't smoke.

Although it would be nice to report that my sojourn at Hayden Hall planted the seedlings of short stories and novels, it wouldn't be true. The hotel may have been rich in material, but I didn't have the tools to mine it. I didn't just lack curiosity; I couldn't—strange as it might sound—make the leap from my surroundings to the blank page in front of me. In effect, I took the hotel and its residents at face value. If the tenants were old and dull, they must have always been old and dull. If one wore a cowbell around his neck—well, he wore a cowbell around his neck. It didn't occur to me to ask why he wore it or how he managed to end up in Hayden Hall. What kind of fiction writer behaves like this?

Virginia Woolf, whose novel *To the Lighthouse* I would pick up just to be soothed by its rhythms, noted in *A Writer's Diary*, "The truth is, people scarcely care for each other. They have this insane instinct for life. But they never become attached to anything outside themselves." Woolf overcame this lack of concern when she became a novelist, almost as if the world of the imagination allowed her to care for people, fictive though they were. I, however, wasn't cut out to care for people I could not touch. What's more, I could not understand those I *could* touch. I didn't lack empathy; I simply could not access the internal workings of other minds. I could outline a plot, take a character from point A to point B, but the interior life—the emotional underpinnings that account for behavior—eluded me.

And yet I wanted to write novels, and did: three of them, to be exact. None was fit for publication and none was much good. The characters I created didn't, as they say, spring to life. Their voices were my voice in different registers, and their behaviors seemed to follow from the plot instead of driving it. For fiction to breathe, a writer has to write about life as though he or she were actually creating it, but the stories that I wrote had less to do with the life I was leading than with the books I was reading. Still, I considered myself a writer in the realist tradition. I wasn't interested in the works of Barth, Pynchon, or Donald Barthleme. I was old-school: I aspired to the Conradian, the Dostoevskian, the Joyce of *The Dubliners*.

And that was the problem: I was too caught up with novels to write a proper one myself. Whatever I wrote smacked of the authors I had read, and though I managed to work in themes and ideas that interested me, I couldn't break the hold of the great novelists. And the odd thing is, I didn't know I wasn't cut out to be a novelist until I began to write a novella in the late Seventies about a writer who lived in a seedy hotel on Manhattan's Upper West Side. It was only then I realized that I knew practically nothing about the people who lived there.

Let me amend that: I did know something about one of the tenants, although it was not information I went out of my way to find. It was handed to me on a small china plate with, if I recall correctly, pale blue filigree. And since it's the only story that I took away from the hotel, I have never forgotten it. The woman who handed me the plate—let's call her Mrs. Hawthorne—was probably closer to eighty than seventy. She was a soft-spoken, diminutive woman, always neatly attired in jacket and skirt, with a string of pearls. Her perfect manners, her perfectly coiffed, perfectly white hair, and her faint Midwestern accent made her an oddity among the hotel's dispirited residents. She was also, as it happened, a theater buff. Two or three times a week, after returning from a show, she would stop by the front desk and run through the highlights with me. Broadway even then was expensive, and what I knew about Sondheim's *Follies* or *The Sunshine Boys*, I learned from Mrs. Hawthorne.

That was the extent of our relationship, until one afternoon when she asked me—as I was walking out of the hotel—if I could change a light bulb in her room. Of course I agreed, but with a certain reluctance. I tried to steer clear of the occupied rooms if I could help it, because it was too sad to enter them. It was one thing for a twenty-four-year-old writer to live in a poorly furnished room; it was quite another for someone over fifty to do so. But when Mrs. Hawthorne opened her door, I saw I had nothing to worry about. True, the room was small and spiked by the inevitable sink and medicine cabinet, but there were also delicately colored lampshades, a small oriental rug, two red-cushioned chairs, a cherrywood table, and a tall armoire. Lace curtains covered the windows; glass and ivory knickknacks rested on the table and dresser; and fine lithographs jostled each other on pale cream walls.

Apologizing for putting me to so much trouble, Mrs. Hawthorne needlessly steadied a chair as I climbed up and changed the bulb. She prepared tea, and afterward we sat facing each other, our knees almost touching. I sipped the tea and looked around—at the elegant surroundings—and realized with a small shock that Mrs. Hawthorne could live anywhere she chose to, and the strangeness of it made me ask why she remained in the hotel.

Mrs. Hawthorne fluttered her hands without replying. She picked up her cup, drank delicately, put it down—then said softly: "I fell in love here."

I don't know what I said to this, but I must have asked or looked a question. Anyway, this is the story she told me:

Mrs. Hawthorne had come to New York from Michigan during the Depression with the idea of becoming a graphic designer. She knew no one and had little money, so she moved into the hotel, which at the time was a perfectly suitable residence for a single woman. The people who lived in Hayden Hall were more or less respectable men and women who held down jobs and took care of their appearance. Mrs. Hawthorne's room was the same one that I was now sitting in, and when she had first moved in, there had lived down the hall, in one of the two-room "suites," a professional gambler by the name of Alfred Bendel (not his real name). Alfred was probably around fifty when he began to court the twenty-something Mrs. Hawthorne, but she didn't mind because Alfred was every inch a gentleman: polite, considerate, well dressed. He was quite stylish, in fact, and Mrs. Hawthorne, like a certain Daisy Buchanan, was taken by the sight of a man's beautiful clothes.

Mrs. Hawthorne was a small-town girl, and Alfred was a New Yorker, a man welcomed by name in many of the better restaurants and night clubs. He took her to the track, to speakeasies, and jazz clubs. It was all very exciting and prompted her infatuation with Broadway. She liked Alfred and thought he liked her as well. She also thought, at first, that she would have to ward off his advances, but Alfred maintained his distance, giving her nothing more than a chaste kiss goodnight when they got off the elevator. Mrs. Hawthorne attributed this to the difference in their ages and thought it was charming that Albert was so formal, so polite. But after they had been seeing each other for some months, Mrs. Hawthorne decided to speak up. One evening, she announced that she liked him and "didn't care a fig" for how old he was and that he shouldn't think about it either. Her openness, however, did not have the desired effect. It wasn't the difference in their ages, he told her, and then he changed the subject. Surprised and somewhat worried, she insisted that he tell her what was bothering him.

Was it her fault? Was it something about her that kept him from becoming, as she put it, "more intimate"? Finally he caved in. With some embarrassment, Alfred confessed that he had peculiar tastes. Truth was he liked to be beaten, to be hit with a knotted rope, to have women walk on his back with spiked heels. He kept a whip in his closet and also a broomstick that could be used to whack the back of his legs.

Well, this, of course, put matters in another light. She considered ending things—but then, on reflection, decided that that would be unfair. What had Alfred done that warranted her disapproval? He had only been good to her, had never asked for anything in return, and, in fact, wasn't asking anything from her now. She decided not to hurt his feelings. She decided to make him happy. Of course, she wasn't adept at it, not in the beginning, but with practice she learned to whip him and beat him and walk across his back in high heels just as he liked. Sometimes his back would be such an awful mass of cuts and welts that they would have to wait a week before starting up again. They continued this way for six or seven years and then one day his heart gave out.

I believe I now interjected: "You mean during the . . . uh . . . the . . ."

Mrs. Hawthorne shook her head. Alfred, she said, had suffered a heart attack while cutting into a steak at Sardi's. He was dead by the time the ambulance arrived. A few weeks later, Mrs. Hawthorne learned that she was his sole beneficiary: he had left her more than two hundred thousand dollars, which was a great deal of money back then. "I see," I said, glancing at the lithographs and bric-a-brac. But I didn't. Patting her perfectly white hair, Mrs. Hawthorne looked me in the eye and said softly: "You see, dear, it pays to be nice to people."

That, after ten months, was what I learned at Hayden Hall. I also learned that I didn't want to live there anymore. After so much time, I wasn't a writer or former graduate student; I was a night watchman in a seedy hotel. The pose of urban anthropologist I had affected had worn thin, and the hotel was beginning to get me down. Sartre was wrong (he was wrong about a lot): hell isn't other people. Other people may be hell, but hell itself must be solitary to be perfect torment. It's purgatory that is other people, a waiting room occupied by men and women whose shoulders create no emotional friction, where familiarity never turns into concern or affection. The hotel's floating population now seemed normal to me. I didn't identify with them, but it did occur to me that if luck took a hand and smacked me with it, I might also end up a middle-aged man living alone in a furnished room, eating Thanksgiving dinner in a Greek coffee shop along upper Broadway. How hard could it be to fall into my own solitary half-mad groove of life?

In late December, I gave notice. Sas shrugged. "Don't come back," he told me, not unkindly. The first day of the New Year, I took my savings and headed south to finish my novel, and when the money ran out I got a job on a construction crew outside Charleston, South Carolina. I continued to drift and to take a number of jobs, though none that ever kept me up past midnight. But after a while I lost my patience for physical labor and for writing uneven novels. Actually, I came to realize that the fiction I wrote didn't measure up to the fiction I was reading; and why would I want to be a cut-rate John Cheever or a dullish Peter Taylor?

This, of course, doesn't stop people from writing fiction (or poetry), but it did me. Not only could I not comprehend the emotional lives of other people—at least not to the extent of envisioning what their feelings might lead them to do—I couldn't rid myself of the sound and sense of the novelists I admired. In effect, my inability to free myself from the Great Books prevented me from acquiring a voice that, for better or worse, was my own. By the same token, this feeling for literary prose still made me want to write sentences. So I suppose you could say that my weakness as a novelist became my strength as an essayist. This is, of course, both too shapely and reductive a statement; and yet a day arrived when it seemed more natural to write about books than to write one myself.

In time, if you attend to the self, temperament prevails. At some point in my early thirties (after I failed at writing my novella about Hayden Hall), I came to the conclusion that literature mattered; I, not so much. So I took a job in publishing and began writing criticism and essays. As for the hotel, I heard that sometime in the mid-Eighties, the air rights had been sold for half a million dollars and a few years later the building itself. Sas died ten or twelve years ago, and sometimes I think of him when the 79th Street cross-town bus turns West from Columbus Avenue. And sometimes I think of the switchboard and of the man with the cowbell, and I wonder if he's still wearing it and if he takes it off when he goes to sleep.

CREDITS

"When Writers Speak" appeared in abbreviated form in *The New York Times Book Review*, September 25, 2009.

"Carpe Noctem: A Little Night Music," *The New Yorker*, May 30, 2005.

"Slang-Whanger: William Hazlitt's Impetuous Prose," *The New Yorker*, May 18, 2009.

"Too True: The Art of the Aphorism," *Harper's*, February, 2008.

"The Usual Suspect: Edgar Allan Poe, Consulting Detective," *Harper's*, January, 2007.

"A Man for All Reasons: Jacques Barzun" appeared in altered form as "Age of Reason" in *The New Yorker*, October 22, 2007.

"En Garde: the Duel in History," *The New Yorker*, March 12, 2007.

"Some Remarks on the Pitfalls of Biography: Especially Where Writers Are Concerned," unpublished ms.

"Slow Fade: F. Scott Fitzgerald in Hollywood," *The New Yorker*, November 16, 2009.

"The Worst of Times: Revisiting the Great Depression," *Harper's*, November, 2009.

"The Long Goodbye: *The Sixties—In Pace Requiem,*" *Harper's*, October, 2008.

"The Night Man—or Why I'm Not a Novelist," unpublished ms.